The Art of Drama

A Streetcar Named Desire

Published by Peripeteia Press Ltd.

First published September 2023

ISBN: 978-1-913577-88-9

Check out our A-level English Literature website, peripeteia.webs.com

PERIPETEIA PRESS

Contents

Introduction to *The Art of Drama* series

The philosopher Nietzsche described his work as 'the greatest gift that [mankind] has ever been given' while the Elizabethan poet Edmund Spenser hoped his book *The Faerie Queene* [1590] would magically transform readers into noblemen. Two hundred years later Wordsworth and Coleridge hoped their *Lyrical Ballads* [1798] would radically improve English sensibilities. In comparison, our aims for *The Art of Drama* series of books are a little more modest. Fundamentally, we aim to provide books that will be of maximum interest and usefulness to students of English and to their teachers.

In this new series of books, we aim to reproduce the success of our *The Art of Poetry* series by providing fine-grained, well-informed, lively and engaging material on the key issues in key drama set texts. In the first book in the series, we focused on J. B. Priestley's popular old stager, *An Inspector Calls*. In the second, we turned our critical attention to Shakespeare's notoriously dark and troubling Scottish play, *Macbeth*. Other titles in the series comprise of guides to three other Shakespearean tragedies *Romeo and Juliet*, *Hamlet* and *Othello* as well as guide to a modern play, *Jerusalem*, by Jez Butterworth.

As with all our poetry books, we hope this new series will appeal to English teachers as well as students of Literature. There is a plethora of material already available on Williams' *Streetcar...* on the market. However, many books aimed at GCSE pupils present information in condensed, broken up or broken down, note and bullet pointed formats. A distinguishing feature of our critical guides is that they are, fundamentally, comprised of a series of short essays. Examination boards require GCSE students to write essays, yet rarely are they encouraged to read literary essays, not least because there's a paucity of this sort of material pitched at this age group. Although there is academic material on *A Streetcar Named Desire*, little of this is written specifically for GCSE or A-level students. Hence, we have tried to fill this significant gap with essays modelling how to engage critically with Literary.

texts.

With the ever-increasing demands and importance of terminal exams, there's a great pressure on students and teachers to reach top grades. One way to attempt to do this is to drill students with exam technique and fill their heads with information in the hope that they will be able to regurgitate it accurately. In our opinion, that sort of factory production-line approach to learning cuts the heart out of the experience of reading and writing about literature, i.e., the forming of our own critical views and feelings. Good critical writing about poems, novels and plays does not merely regurgitate somebody else's ideas uncritically, rather it expresses the critical opinions of the writer, informed, of course, by their experiences in the classroom and elsewhere. No two essays on any Literary text should be exactly the same. Ideally, English teaching should nurture pupils' ability to express their own critical thinking about texts in their own emerging critical voices, informed by discussion with peers and the expertise of teachers.

Our essays in this collection do not follow any specific framework or aim to hit specific assessment objectives. We are not trying to get in 12.5% of context or to make sure we always finish with a telling quote. Rather the writers of this guide have been given free rein to write about what they find most interesting about their chosen topics, whether this be a central theme, character or scene. It is our conviction that when we write about the things that most interest us, we write our best work.

This new guide to *Streetcar...* [as for economy we will call it] is aimed primarily at GCSE students aiming for the highest grades and at A-level English Literature students, as well as teachers and lecturers. Some sections of the guide will be valuable to pupils at both key stages, but others, such as the material on the critical reception of the play over time will be most useful to A-level students. Our material seeks to stimulate a critical response, which might include fervent agreement or even strong disagreement. We aim to encourage students to think critically, to reflect, compare and evaluate different critical views as part of the essential process of formulating their own.

Recently, in her biography of the metaphysical poet and theologian, John Donne, Katherine Rundell wrote that 'to read the full text of a Donne sermon is a little like mounting a horse only to discover that it is an elephant: large and unfamiliar'.[1] We hope that if you expect that reading this guide will be akin to riding a donkey or perhaps an ox, you'll be as surprised as Rundell to discover it is a winged horse, and hopefully delighted too.

Introduction to *A Streetcar Named Desire*

Although Williams' earlier play, *The Glass Menagerie* had garnered some critical acclaim and enjoyed a long run at New York's Playhouse Theatre, it was *A Streetcar Named Desire*, first performed on December 3, 1947, that really made Williams' name as a playwright and established him in the first rank of post-war American writers. An immediate smash hit, its first performance was received with a 30-minute standing ovation.

Before settling on the now iconic title of the play, Williams had various other working alternatives, including *The Passion of a Moth*, Blanche's *Chair to the*

Moon, *The Primary Colours* and *Electric Avenue*. The superiority of a title he only seems to have decided on at the very last moment seems obvious to us now. For one thing, there really was a streetcar serving the French Quarter of New Orleans called 'Desire', so the title roots the play in the real world. Additionally, 'streetcar' suggests a journey, while the pleasures and torments of 'desire' are a major thematic concern of the play. Several critics have also suggested that its combination of the concrete vehicle with the abstract emotion, the title sets up the series of binaries on which the rest of the play is pegged.

In his introductory essay to the Penguin Classics edition of the play, writing in 2004, fellow American playwright, Arthur Miller, emphasised how he knew from the first minutes of watching the first production of *Streetcar...* that it

---

[1] Katherine Rundell, *Super-Infinite, The Transformations of John Donne*.

opened up new possibilities for what could be depicted on the American stage: 'the play and the production had thrown open doors to another theatre world'. Miller opined that it was not some kind of structural ingenuity that made the play striking, rather it was the 'writing itself that left one excited and elevated'. Remarkable, in particular, according to Miller was the play's distinctively rich language, which seemed to flow from the 'writer's soul' as a 'single voice' while, 'remarkably', at the same time, allowing each character to have their own distinctive speech patterns.

Williams' play is now widely considered to be one of the greatest of American dramas, featuring some of the most compelling characters ever written for the stage. Fellow writer, Alfred Uhry claims that it also contains 'the finest dialogue ever written for an American play.'

Writing about plays

The play and the novel

Plays and novels have several significant features in common, such as characters, dialogue, plots and settings. In addition, students read plays in lessons, often sitting at desks in the same way as they read novels. So, it's not surprising that many students treat these two related, but distinct, literary art forms as if they were the same thing. Though sometimes this can be just a slip of the pen, often this error is a good indicator of a weak grasp of the nature of the text. Stronger responses fully appreciate the fact that *Streetcar...* is a play, written for the stage by a playwright and realise the implications of the writer's choice to tell their story through the dramatic form. We can track some of these implications by considering the different opportunities for characterisation and settings provided by the page and the stage.

Characterisation

Imagine you're a novelist writing a scene introducing a major character. Survey the rich variety of means at your disposal: You could begin with a quick pen portrait of their appearance using your narrative voice, or you could have your characters say or do something significant. Alternatively, you could utilise your narrator to provide comments about, and background on, the character. Then again, you might take us into the character's thoughts and reveal what's really going on inside their head. If you're trying to convey thought as it happens you could use a stream of consciousness.

Now imagine that you're a playwright introducing a major character. Consider the far more limited means at your disposal. Though you could describe a character's appearance, you'd have to communicate this through stage directions, which, of course, a theatre audience would not be able to read or hear. The same holds true for background information and narratorial style comments about the character, none of which would an audience be able to read. Unless you are going to use the dramatic devices known as the aside and the soliloquy, as Shakespeare famously used in his great tragedies, you will struggle to find a direct way to show what your character's thinking. As a playwright, stage action and dialogue, however, are your meat and drink. While for a novelist being able to write cracking dialogue is a useful part of the repertoire, for a dramatist it's the sine qua non.

In general, as a visual and aural medium, drama focuses our attention on the outward behaviour of characters. Skilfully done, this can, of course, also reveal their interior thoughts. Nevertheless, novels more easily present the workings of the mind. You may have noticed this when novels are adapted into films and directors have to make the decision about whether to use a voiceover to convey the narrators' or characters' thoughts. Rarely does this work well.

Settings

With a swish of his or her fountain pen or deft fingers running over a keyboard, a novelist can move quickly and painlessly from one setting to another. One chapter of a novel could be set in a medieval village, the next on a far distant planet in the far distant future. The only limitation is the novelist's skill in rendering these worlds. What is true for geographical settings is also true for temporal ones. A novelist can write 'One thousand years later...' or track a character from cradle to grave. A novelist can also play around with narrative time, using flashbacks and flashforwards. While chapter one of our exemplar novel might begin in 1972 in a small seaside village in Cornwall, chapter two might switch to a trench on the frontline during the WWI and chapter three take us all the way back to Ancient Athens. Chapter four might be set in contemporary Baghdad. And so on.

Though a little more restricted, a modern film director can also move fairly easily between geographical and temporal settings and can crosscut between them. But not so a playwright. Why? Because plays are written for an actual physical stage and radically changing a stage set during the action of a play is a tricky, potentially cumbersome business. Imagine a medieval village, with its ramshackle thatched huts, pig pens and dirty streets. How are you going to transform this stage set to the dizzyingly futuristic world of Planet Zog in 2188 A.D. without the audience noticing?

Possibly stage technicians could dismantle and construct the different stage sets while the audience waits patiently for the action to restart. More likely you'd use a break, perhaps between the scenes or, better, during the interval for any major re-arrangement of stage scenery. Practically speaking, how many different stage sets could you create for a single play? Minimalistic stage designs might allow you to employ more settings, but you'd still be far more restricted than a film director or a novelist. And then there's the expense of building elaborate sets. Theatres aren't usually flush with money and complex stage sets are likely to be expensive. Another way out of this problem would be to have a pretty much bare and unchanging stage set and convey changes in scenes through the dialogue, a technique Shakespeare used for The Globe stage. Think, for instance, of the start of *The Tempest*, where the action of the opening scene takes place on a boat out a sea or in *Hamlet* where the opening scene is supposed to be taking place on the battlements of Elsinore castle in the middle of the night.

Here's our version of this sort of minimalist, setting-through-dialogue technique:

Stage direction: Two characters meet on a bare stage.
Character 1: What is this strange, futuristic place with extraordinary buildings?
Character 2: Why, this is the capital city of the Planet Zog.
Character 1: Aha! And, unless I'm mistaken, the year is now 2188 A.D.
etc.

As we'll see, professional playwrights tend to do this sort of scene setting with a tad more subtlety.

The action in plays also tends to take place in chronological order, with time moving forward in a fairly regular, linear direction. Partly this is because as we watch plays in real time, it would be difficult to convey to an audience that a particular scene was actually a flashback. There are exceptions, of course, to the chronological trend. Notably Harold Pinter's *Betrayal*, for instance, in which the action of the play unfolds backwards from the present to past.

The time frame of a play also tends to be limited – days, weeks, perhaps even months, but very rarely years, decades or centuries. After all, it's not easy for an actor, or series of actors, to convincingly present characters ageing over a prolonged period. Additionally, as Aristotle suggested, a tight time span can amplify the intensity of the drama.

The stage and the page

Few writers excel in both the novel and the play as literary forms [Samuel Beckett, Anton Chekhov and Michael Frayn come to mind] which underlines the point about the different demands of writing for the stage and for the page. Novels take place in the reader's mind or ear; plays take place in an actual physical space on an actual physical stage. For the latter to happen, a whole load of people other than the writer have to be involved – directors, actors, designers, producers, technicians and so forth. This takes us to the heart of another crucial difference between reading a play, reading a novel and seeing a play on a stage. When we're reading a novel, the novelist can fill in the details of what is happening around the dialogue, such as gestures made by the characters:

'Did they even have pigpens in medieval villages?' asked Mikey, cocking his left eyebrow in a typically quizzical manner.

When we **read** a play, as in a classroom, sometimes these details are apparent from stage directions. However, on the page we cannot see what characters are doing while other characters are speaking. So it's easy for us to forget that silent characters are present in a scene and that their presence may significantly affect the action. When we **watch** a play, however, the actors on stage reveal how their characters are reacting to the scene and these reactions often convey crucial information about relationships, feelings and atmosphere. What, for example, how do Steve, Pablo and Mitch respond to the entrance of Stella and Blanche during the late-night poker game in Scene 3. We know they don't rise, politely, as gentleman are supposed to do when ladies enter a room, as Stanley tells us so. But we don't know whether they look up, smile, make any eye contact or ignore the women and remain fully focused on their cards. Similarly, what are Steven and Pablo doing while Mitch becomes interested in Blanche and then Stanley grows increasingly furious in the same scene? Directors and the actors would have to decide how these two characters react to what's going on, as nothing in the playscript tells us. Reading in this creative way, we become directors of our own productions of *Streetcar*....

Without the visual dimension of the stage, it is easy for readers to ignore the things that are supposed to be happening in the narrative background while each character is speaking. If a play on a page is similar to a musical score awaiting performance, a play on the stage is the full concert.

Appreciation of the differences between a novel and a play, helps students to notice the key skills of the playwright. And focusing on the dramatic devices used by a playwright has a double benefit: firstly, all good analytical literary essays concentrate on the writer's craft; secondly, such a focus emphasises to the examiner that students understand the nature of the type of text they are exploring, viz. a play, and distinguishes them from other readers who don't really appreciate this fact.

The nature of the play

What is a tragedy?

The exact nature of the literary genre we call 'tragedy' is much debated. According to *The Complete A-Z English Literature Handbook* a tragedy is a 'drama which ends disastrously' and falls into two broad types:

- Greek tragedy, where fate brings about the downfall of the character[s].
- Shakespearean tragedy, where a character has free will and their fatal flaw causes the downfall.

According to Jennifer Wallace in *The Cambridge Introduction to Tragedy*, 'Tragedy is an art form created to confront the most difficult experiences we face; death, loss, injustice, thwarted passion, despair'. Wallace goes on to explain that 'questions about the causes of suffering, which are raised in each culture, are posed powerfully in tragedy'.[2] That's helpful, but couldn't we say the same sorts of things about the academic subjects of philosophy and religious studies?

While, on the one hand, there are critics, such as Terry Eagleton, who argue

---

[2] Wallace, *The Cambridge Introduction to Tragedy*.

the only thing that the plays we label as tragedies have in common is that they are 'very, very sad', on the other, many critics opine that all literary tragedies share common, distinctive formal features which separate them from real-life stories of great unhappiness. One of the first and most influential theorists of tragedy was Aristotle.

Aristotle

Often it is assumed that Aristotle was setting down a prescriptivist rulebook for writing tragedies, a kind of classical instruction manual for aspiring playwrights to follow slavishly. This assumption is mistaken. In fact, Aristotle, in his *Poetics*, was describing the features of classical tragedies as he saw them. Taken as prescriptivist or descriptivist, what is certain is that Aristotle's ideas about tragedies have been massively influential. In particular, four key ideas have helped shape the ways tragedies have been written, performed and read for hundreds of years. These ideas concern:

i.   the nature of the protagonist
ii.   the cause of tragic action
iii. the significance of plot
iv.   the emotional effect of tragedy on an audience.

For our purposes, the first two of these concepts are particularly interesting. The protagonist in classical tragedy is always high-born, a prince or king or someone of equivalent status. This means their fall is as precipitous, destructive and dramatic as possible - right from the top to the very bottom of society [imagine an elephant falling off a skyscraper] in a way that the fall of someone from the bottom to the bottom of society [imagine a mouse falling off a kerb] would not be. As the tragic hero or heroine is high-born and they fall a long way down, the impact of their fall causes immense damage to society, sending shockwaves out across the whole world of the play, creating cracks and fissures across the social landscape. Crucially, according to Aristotle, the primary cause of the fall is a fault in the tragic protagonist. Historically Shakespearean critics often conceived of this tragic flaw, or hamartia, in character-based or psychological terms.

Is *Streetcar* a tragedy?

According to Roxanna Stuart, an actor who played Blanche, 'the first four scenes are comedy; then come two scenes of elegy, mood, romance, then five scenes of tragedy'.[3] Perhaps Stuart is right. But the balance of comic, elegiac and tragic elements probably depends on the way the play is acted and directed. Overall, although there are only passing references to death in *A Streetcar Named Desire* [Allan's suicide, the deaths of the DuBois relatives and the Spanish flower seller's cries of 'Flores para los muertos'], and nobody actually dies at the end, it would be difficult to argue that the play isn't tragic. How it ends is, of course, crucial. For many of us, the displacement of Blanche to an asylum, accompanied by the 'inhuman sobs' of her sister, as well as Mitch, are probably enough to justify this description. If you take into account the indifference of the poker players at the end, and Eunice's resignation to a life of self-delusion - 'you've got to keep on going' - and the fact that Stanley has completely 'got away with' raping his sister-in-law, then the play does indeed come across as bleak, at the very least. Critics like Philip Smithers have made some interesting comparisons between *A Streetcar Named Desire* and Shakespeare's tragedy *Hamlet*, suggesting that in both plays the tragedy lies in the 'collision between two world views'[4]. According to Gillian Anderson, who played Blanche in 2014, audiences have frequently left playhouses in floods of tears after watching it. Certainly, the ending of *A Streetcar Named Desire* is not comic.

What arguably is a little less clear, however, is whether we can actually label *Streetcar...* as a tragedy in the Greek or Shakespearean mould. As we've noted, in Greek tragedy, fate dictates the protagonist's downfall; in Shakespearean tragedy it is brought about by the character's 'fatal flaw' or hamartia. The latter would seem to describe *Streetcar...* more accurately: Blanche's capacity to deceive herself, as well as her vanity and penchant for flirting with young men, would certainly seem to be worthy of that description. Furthermore, it is quite difficult to attribute the tragic ending of the play to

---

[3] *The Cambridge Companion to Tennessee Williams*, p.48.

[4] *Williams and Will: Worlds Colliding in Hamlet and A Streetcar Named Desire*, Emag Plus 75.

fate, unless we interpret that term in a more modern and post WW2 way and define 'fate' as the socioeconomic circumstances in which Blanche finds herself in 1940s New Orleans, arguably a situation over which she has very little control.

This way of viewing the play is perhaps more productive, as it redirects the focus away from just one individual - Blanche - and encourages us to see her in the context of the 1940s setting. If we identify Blanche and Stanley as representatives of the Old and New way of life in the American South after the war, then Blanche is, at least in part, the victim of circumstances: she is a woman, she has no independent means and she belongs to that dying breed of wealthy Scarlett O'Hara-esque landowners whose demise characterised the late nineteenth and early twentieth century in America.

The other advantage to viewing the play through this more modern lens is that it allows us to assess the nature of the play in terms of the other characters who are, in most cases, also tragic in their own ways. Although Stella is not taken away to a lunatic asylum at the end of the play, and the birth of her baby might be seen as a symbol of hope, she does have to sacrifice her only remaining blood relative, tolerate physical abuse at the hands of her husband and accept that he may have raped her sister. Stella might be very different from her sister, but she is equally constrained by her gender at a time when it was still very much a man's world. As Simon Bubb has suggested, 'the real pathos at the end of A Streetcar Named Desire derives mostly from Stella's torment about the implications of the choice she has made'.[5] Similarly, Mitch, who is also left sobbing regretfully in the final scene, seems destined for a life of loneliness and grief. Perhaps the only main character to come out of the play intact, even stronger, is Stanley, the wife beating rapist. That's quite a pessimistic ending in its own right.

Southern Gothic

Southern Gothic is a sub-genre of Gothic Literature that developed in America

---

[5] A Tragedy of the Powerless, EMC magazine.

in the nineteenth century. Characteristics of the sub-genre include odd-ball, transgressive and misfit characters, madness, obsession and weirdly skewed desires, haunted, insular landscapes and sinister, decaying buildings and macabre storylines, all shot through an underlying and all-pervasive sense of decay, alienation and angst.

Twice Blanche mentions one of the most significant writers in the Southern Gothic tradition, Edgar Allan Poe, and Williams' play certainly has shades of the Southern Gothic about it. Most obvious is outcast Blanche's and her

mental distress, her retreat into fantasies and her alcoholism. Her description of the loss of Belle Reeve in Scene 1 and the 'long parade to the graveyard' is distinctly Gothic. So too is the climax of the last scene, when Blanche's distressed and disordered state of mind is projected as nightmarish noises and shadows. The eerie blind Mexican vendor with her flowers for the dead, is another obviously Gothic element.

The Southern Gothic 'brings to light the extent to which the idyllic vision of the pastoral, agrarian South rests on the massive repressions of the region's historical realities: slavery, racism and patriarchy'.[6] As a faded and corrupted Southern Belle Blanche who tries to cover up her corruption, Blanche is a walking embodiment of the key concern of the Sothern Gothic.

---

[6] Article form Oxford Research Encyclopedias.

The Playwright

'I write out of love for the South ... once a way of life that I am just old enough to remember – not a society based on money... I write about the South because I think the war between romanticism and the hostility to it is very sharp there.'

Thomas Lanier Williams was born in Columbus, Mississippi in March 1911. HIs early childhood was spent living with his maternal grandparents in their expansive, rural house. His grandfather was an Episcopalian minister but despite this, he was quite a liberal man whose home was a safe haven for the young Tom, his mother and his siblings, Rose and Dakin.

At the age of eight, Tom and the family were uprooted from the relaxed, genteel surroundings of Clarksdale when his father, previously a travelling salesman, took a job at a shoe factory in St. Louis. Cornelius Williams was an abusive man who drank heavily and was prone to violence. According to some commentators, Tom's mother, Edwina adopted the manners and style of Southern Belle, telling her son not to 'hang back with the brutes'. Unsurprisingly, some critics suggest that Edwina was the inspiration for Blanche Dubois. The playwright's sister, Rose, became increasingly erratic until she was diagnosed with schizophrenia as a young woman. It is likely that she spoke out against her father's sexual abuse of her. She was subjected to a frontal lobotomy in 1943 which left her infantilised and institutionalised for the rest of her life. Tom was devastated by her condition and is thought to have become increasingly dependent on drugs and alcohol as a result of his sister's brutal treatment. Williams once claimed that the 'one major theme' in his work was 'the destructive power of society on the sensitive nonconformist individual', vulnerable and sensitive individuals like his sister Rose who he described as the 'most beautiful creature on God's green earth'.

From 1929 Williams attended The University of Missouri but it was not a success; he disliked his classes and failed to fit in with the fraternity atmosphere. Eventually his father insisted that he get a job in the shoe factory which Williams hated so much that he redoubled his efforts to write and despite another false start at Washington University in St. Louis, he eventually graduated from The University of Iowa. Around 1939 he adopted the name Tennessee.

It took Tennessee Williams several years to gain a foothold as a writer. In the late 1930s he was forced to take menial jobs to support himself but in 1939 he received a grant of $1000 from the Rockefeller Foundation. This brought him to the attention of MGM films where he was given a short contract as a screenplay writer for $250 a week.

Williams' most prolific period came between 1944 - 1959. His first successful play *The Glass Menagerie* was concerned with a declassed family consisting of a domineering mother with a cynical son who tries to find a husband for his mentally fragile sister who retreats into a fantasy world with her collection of glass animals. *The Glass Menagerie* won the New York Drama Critics' Circle Award and paved the way for the smash hit which was *A Streetcar Named Desire* in 1947. Director Elia Kazan brought the play to the silver screen and a number of Williams' plays, such a *Cat on A Hot Tin Roof*, were also turned into major feature films.

Williams' personal life was always turbulent. Throughout his twenties he struggled to come to terms with being gay. At the time and throughout much of his life, homosexuality was seen as 'deviant' and synonymous with mental illness. Mainstream society was opposed to any expression of sexuality which it deemed to be abnormal, and this concern is evident in much of Williams' writing. His homosexuality, alongside his left-leaning political convictions, also contributed to his sense that he was on the outside of a hostile and unjust mainstream society. Unsurprisingly, in his writing Williams expresses a deep sense of solidarity with various outsiders, outcasts and underdogs.

Blanche, of course, is run out of town for being promiscuous and is eventually incarcerated for speaking out about Stanley's rape. Blanche also married a gay man, Allan Grey, who struggled to cope with the harsh realities of mainstream society. Blanche was clearly an innocent at the time and when she admits to having 'failed him in some mysterious way', it isn't difficult to assume that the marriage was never consummated and her promiscuity arose, perhaps, from a need for self-validation. Another example is Brick from *Cat on a Hot Tin Roof*. Brick is tormented by his love and guilt surrounding his friend Skipper and although the conventions of the time prevented Williams from being explicit about their relationship, it is clear to the audience what is going on.

Williams' relationships were also fraught with difficulty. Following a number of short-lived encounters, in 1945 he met the volatile Pancho Rodríguez y González. The two stayed together for several years until Williams ended the relationship in 1947. Williams' next long-term relationship was with Frank Merlo. The relationship lasted for 14 years and even after it ended, Williams nursed Merlo, who died of lung cancer in 1963. There was a degree of stability in this relationship; Merlo took charge of Williams' domestic and professional arrangements, but drugs, alcohol and affairs brought the arrangement to an end. As a gay man, Williams was deeply worried about ageing and losing his appeal to younger men, but in his sixties he had an affair with a young writer named Robert Carroll.

Tragically, Tennessee Williams' latter years were marked by prescription drug abuse and alcoholism. Often, it seems, he feared that he might go mad, describing this permanent fear as the 'monkey on his back' that never goes away. But Williams also accepted that the emotional turbulence of his personal life, his fury at the injustices of society and his sometimes almost paranoid state of mind were the fuel he needed to power his work.

However, he never recaptured the heady days of the 40s and 50s and his later work was largely unsuccessful. Williams died on 25 February 1983 in his suite in the Hotel Elysée in New York. Although his death was initially recorded as being from the accidental inhalation of a bottle cap, it was later found to have been from a fatal dose of a sedative. In his will Williams, like Blanche, expressed the desire to be buried at sea.

'I, Thomas Lanier [Tennessee] Williams, being in sound mind upon this subject, and having declared this wish repeatedly to my close friends-do hereby state my desire to be buried at sea. More specifically, I wish to be buried at sea at as close as possible point as the American poet Hart Crane died by choice in the sea... I wish to be sewn up in a canvas sack and dropped overboard.'

Socio-historical context

A Streetcar Named Desire was first performed in 1947, two years after the end of WW2. As such, it reflects a time of enormous social and economic change in America. The end of WW2 brought about an acceleration in a transition which had already begun during the American Civil War [1861-65] and as a result of the Abolition of Slavery in 1865. Gradually the old, southern aristocracy, whose power and wealth had largely been a product of the slave trade, lost much of the privilege it had previously enjoyed. The decline of the South is clearly embodied in the character of Blanche, posing as a 'Southern Belle' and desperately trying to hold on to her dignity and superior social status at a time when most people no longer deferred to class hierarchy. Everything about Blanche's appearance and behaviour smacks of a bygone era: she wears glamorous 'upper-class' clothes, attempts to assert her superiority by using elevated and affected language, and frequently demonstrates her class's old, xenophobic and discriminatory attitudes through her response to Stanley and the conditions in which he and Stella live. By contrast, Stanley is dressed in 'blue denim work clothes', a look that has since become synonymous with blue-collar cool, in brands like Levi's 501 jeans.

Unfortunately for Blanche, by the late 1940s, the old-fashioned southern way of life had begun to change radically. The world that Tennessee Williams depicts so knowledgeably was forward-thinking and diverse, a country in which individuals could confidently pursue their idea of the 'American Dream'. One aspect of this modernisation was industrialisation. Having suffered greatly during the Great Depression of 1929-1939, New Orleans became a thriving hub of industrial activity during WW2, primarily in the making and supplying of military equipment for the war effort. During the war, military bases and factories had been set up all over the south, most of which continued to function after the war and provide ongoing employment for local people, fuelling a rise in rural-urban migration. Furthermore, the southern states of America were a rich source of oil and gas, creating oil millionaires, like the offstage character of Shep Huntleigh, to whom Blanche turns for financial support.

During the twentieth century, and particularly after the war, immigration rates rose dramatically in America as people flocked to the 'land of opportunity' from all over the world in search of freedom and prosperity. As the son of a Polish immigrant, Stanley represents this social shift. Although Blanche refers to him disparagingly as a 'Polack', naively looking down on and trying to assert her superiority over him as an outsider, in fact it is she who does not fit in. In his cast, Williams also includes characters from a range of other heritages, including the Mexican flower seller, Pablo and the Negro woman. Although racial tension was, and would continue to be, hugely problematic in America at this time, Tennessee Williams' New Orleans reflects a uniquely harmonious multicultural community, in which working class immigrants like Stanley could prosper. As a soldier, Stanley had earned the respect of their contemporaries not by being rich slave owners, but by fighting bravely for their country and becoming national heroes.

The end of WW2 also brought about some retrograde changes in attitudes towards gender and sexuality. Although many women had found strength and fulfilment by taking on traditionally male roles during the war, most were expected to return to their pre-war domestic lives in peacetime. While the more conventional gender roles of Stella and Stanley conform to this, clearly Blanche stands out as an example of a woman who does not fit neatly into that stereotype. Up until recently a schoolteacher with her own income, she is not married and has what some might regard as a more masculine and predatory attitude towards sex. Unconventional and different, Blanche is eventually rejected by Mitch and committed to an asylum. Similarly, her former husband Allan Grey has been driven to suicide by society's condemnation of homosexuality, still illegal in America at this time.

Despite presenting us with a post-war world which is indisputably progressive in so many ways, Tennessee Williams shows us that society's attitude to difference in 1940s New Orleans was nevertheless intolerant and exclusive.

Stagecraft

When you're writing about a novel, it's always productive to focus on narration. Narration includes narrative perspective, such as first and third person, types of narrators, such as naïve and unreliable, as well as narrative techniques, such as the use of dialogue, crosscuts and flashbacks. Narration is worth focusing your attention on because it's an integral feature of all novels and short stories. In plays, the equivalent of narration is stagecraft. Stagecraft includes the nature of the stage set as, the utilisation of lighting, music and sound effects and of costumes and props. Examining stagecraft is an incisive and revealing way to explore the playwright at work.

Stage set

As we mentioned in our discussion of the key differences between novels and plays, the latter invariably have fewer settings since dramatic texts have to be physically realised in stage designs. And, as we also noted, changing from one elaborate stage set to another presents problems for directors and, potentially for the finances of a production. What sort of choices does a stage designer have to make when creating a set? Firstly, a lot depends on the nature of the play, as well as the playwright, the director and the budget. Some playwrights are very particular about the settings of their plays and describe them in tremendous detail.

Other playwrights sketch out very specific but minimalistic sets. Samuel Beckett in *Waiting for Godot*, for instance, describes the stage set in the sparest way possible, using just six simple words: 'A country road. A tree. Evening'. Even if the playwright doesn't provide a great deal of information about the exact setting, a director is likely to have an overall concept for a play and insist, albeit to varying degrees, that the set design fits with this. If, for instance, a director wishes to bring out the contemporary political resonances of a play such as *Julius Caesar* she or he might dress the characters like well-known American politicians and set the play in a place looking a little like the modern White House. Similarly, Shakespeare's *Richard III* has often been relocated to an imagined modern fascistic state.

Given free rein, a stage designer must decide how realistic, fantastical, symbolic and/or expressionist their stage set will be. The representation of what looks like the real world on stage, as if the audience are looking in through an invisible fourth wall into a sitting room or such like, is called verisimilitude. It is the equivalent of photographic realism in fine art and is often associated with realist plays. Williams' play is, of course, rooted in a kind of realism, but this is overlaid with a poetic and symbolic quality reflected in the stage directions.

In *Streetcar...* there are two major settings: the rooms within the Kowalski's and the street areas outside it. Sometimes the lighting will focus the audience's attention on one of these two, at others it will switch the focus from one to the other. Sometimes, simultaneously, we can see characters both inside and outside the flat, such as when Stanley listens in to the two sisters' private conversation in Scene 4. Indeed, although the inner settings of the rooms within the flat perform different functions, with the bathroom, for instance, Blanche's choice for a place of refuge, fundamentally the outside spaces are public ones and the inside of the flat a more private space.

Elysian Fields and its surroundings

Famously Williams wrote particularly lyrical stage directions. Those that open. 'warm' breath?

Probably to the relief of the set designer, these rich, lyrical descriptions are, however, grounded in more concrete, physical details. The play begins, the reader is told more matter-of-factly, in front of a 'two-storey building' that is situated in a real place, a specific and actual street in New Orleans, called Elysian Fields. This area is 'poor' and its houses are 'mostly white frame, weathered grey, with rickety outside stairs'. Stanley and Stella's home is in a building which 'contains two flats, upstairs and down'. Linking the two flats are some 'faded white stairs'. Not only are these details easy to imagine and research, they are also fairly easy to reproduce on a stage.

Alongside the lighting, the other most significant specific establishing detail is the reference to music. Two stage devices, lighting and music, will, of course, both prove particularly significant as the action unfolds. Here they both help to generate the mood and atmosphere, a feeling, Williams wishes to evoke. The blueness creates a softness to the light, while also suggesting a gentle melancholy. Additionally, the scene is set suggestively in the 'evening', just as the blue light is giving way to darkness. The references to 'Negro entertainers at a bar-room' playing a 'tinny piano' with 'infatuated fluency' suggest blues music. And, indeed, the light and the music come together in the final evocative description of the 'blue piano', which Williams tells us 'expresses the spirit of the life' of the district.

In the Penguin Modern Classics edition of the play, the instructions for the stage set run on for about half a page. So, what is established here and how will it be relevant to the rest of the play?

Firstly, that, in financial terms, this is a poor, rather down-at-heel neighbourhood whose better, more elegant days are firmly in the past. Situated near the tram-tracks, its once 'white' buildings are described as having been 'weathered' from white to 'grey'. Additionally, a one-family home has now been split into two flats, with a shared bathroom. An impression of neglect and slow deterioration is confirmed by the description of the building's stairs, which are both 'faded' and 'rickety', and later by Williams' reference to a prevailing 'atmosphere of decay'. Nevertheless, the area just about seems to be clinging to its more illustrious, faded past.

The literary name of the street is significant: In classical literature, the Elysian Fields were a paradise where the most favoured of dead heroes resided. So this should be a place fit for heroes. But also for the dead. Despite the urban decay, the area retains a 'raffish charm', and, in the blue light of evening, it still has a 'kind of lyricism', a drawn-out elegance, that might not be so apparent in the starker light of day. 'Raffish' is a telling adjective, as alongside attractiveness, it also hints at something disreputable. It's also a phrase that could be applied to Stanley.

Faded white elegance, attractive but disreputable, softened by gentle half-light. Certainly, that's a description that resonates throughout the play, most obviously, but also surprisingly, connecting this urban setting with Blanche. She, however, doesn't make the connection: when she arrives at Elysian Fields, Blanche is horrified by Stella's home, appalled that her sister has to live there in such reduced circumstances, commenting that only the gloomy Gothic writer Edgar Allen Poe could do its grimness justice.

Secondly, it's a busy, bustling, racially mixed, rather grimy, but also vibrant urban area. Nearby are 'river warehouses' from which emanate the rich smells of 'bananas and coffee' and the business district, whose lights can be seen at night. Around the corner are several lively bars, such as the Four Deuces, perpetually playing blues music. There's also a French Market, a Chinese shop, from which Blanche buys the paper lantern and a Chinese takeaway. From Eunice's comments in Scene 5 and the appearance later of a prostitute, we can infer that there might be a brothel situated above the Four Deuces. Later we hear that there are bowling alleys close by and, somewhere, also a catholic cathedral.

The Flat

Within the outer setting of Elysian Fields is the interior one of Stella and Stanley's flat. We're told that this comprises of only two rooms, a kitchen and a bedroom. So, it's a very small, humble, cramped flat with not much room for a visitor. As the action of the play unfolds in the play-script, we also hear of various bits of furniture filling the limited space – chairs, a kitchen table, a dressing table with a mirror, a bureau with drawers, a stool and so on – adding to the sense of constriction and, potentially, even of claustrophobia. So cramped is the flat, in fact, that Blanche will not have her own room, or any privacy, sleeping instead on a temporary 'folding bed' in the kitchen. There also seems to be a shared bathroom, on the second floor, where Steve and Eunice live. However, there's some ambiguity about the exact location of this bathroom. In Scene 1 the stage directions refer to a 'narrow door' connecting the bedroom to a bathroom, while Stella is also described as going from the kitchen 'into the bathroom' without seeming to climb any stairs and, in Scene 2, Blanche comes straight out of the bathroom and into the kitchen, again without having to come downstairs. It seems, therefore, that there's both a room with a bath in it inside the flat, and a shared toilet on the floor above.

Increasingly the bathroom within the flat will be the place to which Blanche retires to refresh herself, a place of refuge from the troubles of the world. While Stanley is telling his wife about Blanche's recent past in Scene 7, for

instance, the audience hear the sounds of Blanche happily bathing and singing, oblivious to what is going on. Blanche is described as taking baths several times during the action of the playing, a symbol of her intense desire to make herself clean again. The repeated baths, however, suggest how hard it is for her to wash away the past. Indeed, despite her efforts, in Scene 9, Mitch will refuse to marry her, because he thinks she's 'not clean enough to bring in the house' with his mother.

The fact that 'there is no door between' the kitchen where Blanche will sleep and Stanley and Stella's bedroom adds to Blanche's unease and, to the audience, signals the potential for invasions of privacy and of transgressions. The two spaces are separated only by a flimsy curtain. As Felicia Hardison Londré notes, the absence of a door not only 'raises questions of decency', 'perhaps metaphorically' it also 'heralds the ill-defined' in Blanche's 'coming struggles with Stanley over territorial space'.[7]

In Scene 2, we learn there's also an outside porch. This is significant as it provides another outside space close to the main rooms, where any one character can overhear, but not necessarily see what is going on inside the flat. Similarly, characters inside the flat might not be aware of another character on this porch.

Scene 4 opens with Stella lying on her bed, serene, after the tumultuous events of the night before. This large item of the stage furniture is very important and is likely to dominate the

---

[7] *The Cambridge Companion to Tennessee Williams.*

space within the small, cramped bedroom. Scene 9 opens with Blanche sitting on a 'bedroom chair that she has covered with diagonal and green stripes'. When Mitch arrives at the kitchen door, he pushes past Blanche straight to into 'the bedroom'. After Mitch uncouthly 'draws his foot up on the bed', Blanche reprimands him, saying she has put a 'light cover on it' and that she has 'done so much with this place' since she came, making the room 'dainty'. If this scene takes place in Stella and Stanley's bedroom, rather than in the kitchen where we were told at the start of the play Blanche would be sleeping, at some point she must have moved in and taken over this private space, turfing them out and making it her own. If so, when did this usurpation happen? And where do Stella and Stanley sleep now? If this is the case, then perhaps we can sympathise a bit more with Stanley's hostile feelings towards Blanche and his sense that she is a threat to his marriage.

Another important part of the stage set are the large windows of the flat through which comes the light from the outside world. In Scene 8, in particular, the stage directions include detailed references to the sunlight coming from outside the flat and reflected in the windows of buildings in the nearby business district.

Other settings
Belle Reve
Clearly, from Eunice's comments and from Blanche's reaction when she first arrives in Scene 1, the flat is very different from the sisters' family home of Belle Reve. We learn in the play's first scene that Belle Reve is a plantation, so has extensive land, and is some kind of grand mansion, a 'great big place with white columns'. Hence Blanche's shock at how far her sister seems to have come down in the world. Later we're told that even its final, reduced state, Belle Reve had expansive grounds of twenty acres.

As the name implies, there is something a little unreal about Belle Reve, as if it is more an idea of a place than the real thing. Additionally, as the play goes on, it comes associated less with a beautiful dream and more with a terrible nightmare. Whereas New Orleans is full of bustling, dynamic life, Belle Reve becomes associated with corruption, death and quiet despair. It becomes an emblem of the loss of the dream of the Romantic South.

Other settings mentioned that establish the world of the play, but are not shown on stage, include: the shops, bars and bowling alleys near the Kowalski's flat; an amusement park and Lake Pontchartrain; the town of Laurel where Blanche lived and the disreputable Flamingo hotel where she resided for a while.

Lighting

Lighting can be used starkly and boldly, such as in picking out a main character in a bright spotlight, or it can be used more subtly to convey mood and generate atmosphere. Intense white light makes everything look stark. Blue lights help create a sense of coolness, whereas yellows, oranges and reds generate a sense of warmth and even passion. Floor lights can light an actor from beneath, making them look powerful and threatening. Light coming down on them from above can cause an actor to look vulnerable and threatened or even angelic. Changes of lighting between scenes are common ways of changing the pervasive atmosphere and fading out can be symbolically suggestive.

When Blanche first enters Stella and Stanley's flat at the start of Scene 1 and the light goes on 'behind the blind', the colour is described as a gentle 'light blue'. Blanche is comfortable enough with this pale light, until Stella arrives. Having invited her sister to look at her, Blanche suddenly fears what her sister will be able to see in the 'merciless glare' of the light and, distressed, demands that Stella 'turn that over-light off! Turn that off!' Quickly Williams establishes Blanche's fear of bright light and her intense need to keep certain things, such as her aging, concealed.

Williams' stage directions require the lighting to change at various points in the play. In the moment we've just discussed, for instance, when the blue light goes on inside the flat, simultaneously the lighting of the 'surrounding areas dim[s] out', obviously helping to focus our attention on Blanche and the flat's interior. A similar, cinematic effect, only in reverse, is employed at the end of Scene 2, when the lighting of the inner rooms 'fade into darkness' and the outside wall of the house becomes visible.

The lighting and costumes come together to create a striking visual and artistic impression at the start of Scene 3, The Poker Night, set in the kitchen of the flat. The bold, strident colours used here are more expressionistic than naturalistic, as reflected in Williams' stage directions which refer specifically to a painting by Vincent Van Gough, reproduced on the next page.

Vincent Van Gogh, *The Night Cafe*, 1888

What we can't see here, but you can by looking up the painting online, is how strong and vivid the colours in this paining are, a combination of deep red, yellowy golds, leafy and acid greens. Williams writes that the lighting in the play should create a similar sort of 'lurid nocturnal brilliance', with 'raw colours', like in a child's painting. The luridness is created by the combination of the 'yellow linoleum' of the kitchen table, where the card players are assembled, with the light of an electric bulb that has a 'vivid green glass shade'. Enhancing the effect are the costumes worn by the men – 'coloured shirts, solid blues, a purple, a red-and-white check, a light green'. The colours of a prop, 'vivid slices of watermelon' add to the visual intensity. The strong, 'vivid', 'lurid', and 'raw' primary colours express the men's characters, their virile energy and dynamism, and anticipate the primary violence that will shortly burst out of the scene.

Repeatedly Blanche is associated with whiteness and her delicacy compared to a moth. When she first appears in Scene 1, the stage directions tell us that 'her delicate beauty must avoid a strong light'. Hence, the lighting of The Poker Night signals a distinct and powerful threat to Blanche.

At the moment when the scene is revealed and held for the audience's attention in a short 'silence', we can also see the adjacent bedroom, though this is only lit dimly by the light from the kitchen, filtering through the curtains, and from the light of the street outside. It's important, of course, that light is able to penetrate through these curtains.

When Stella and Blanche appear 'around the corner of the building', though that section of the set might be in darkness at the start of the scene, it will need to become lighted, highlighting how our attention is shifted by the lighting from the men to the women and then on to how they interact.

While the poker game continues in the kitchen, Blanche and Stella retire to the bedroom. Despite the close presence of the men in the room next door, Blanche begins to undress, taking off her blouse. The stage directions make it clear that, wearing only a bra, Blanche stands deliberately in the 'light through the portieres' to attract the attention of the men. When Stella warns her that she might be seen, semi-naked, Blanche professes to be unaware of being caught in the light and moves out of it. However, once Stella goes into the bathroom, very deliberately Blanche 'moves back in the streak of light'. Once, in the light she raises her arms and stretches, showing off her figure. When, soon after, Mitch moves into the semi-dimness of the bedroom and strikes a match to allow Blanche to read the inscription on his silver, a small intimate halo of warm light would briefly envelope and bring them together.

Often Williams use of lighting is poetic, symbolic and expressive, rather than realistic. The overheated colours of this scene complementing the stage action are a good example. Another comes after Stanley hurls the phone to the floor. At this point the lights in this part of the stage 'dim out to darkness' while soon after the lights go up on the 'outer walls'. Natural light does not 'dim out' and then return in a short space of time, so this is a deliberate visual effect, here expressing Stanley's feelings of despair. The lights coming back on coincides with him forcing himself out of this despair and going to try to make-up with Stella.

Although Scene 4 takes place almost entirely in the bedroom, there is a reference the light coming in through the outside door, revealing a 'sky of summer brilliance'. With a cinematic effect, the scene 'fades away' at the end of the scene, though, for a moment, it rests on Stanley and Stella embracing with a 'lingering brightness', making a memorable stage picture of intimacy. It also means the actor playing Blanche has been faded out first.

Scene 5 takes place in late afternoon, and the light at the end of the scene has 'faded to dusk'. Gentle, hazy lighting inside the flat is also suggested by the fact that Stella turns on the bedroom light that is now covered by the paper lantern. This dusky light intensifies, becomes 'deeper' when Blanche is alone on stage and close to falling asleep. Ominously, when she wakes there is a 'little glimmer of lightning about the building'.

The pervasive dimness of the lighting in Scene 6 is essential in terms of conveying the intimate mood and atmosphere inside the flat, but also in terms of maintaining Mitch's perceptions of Blanche. Increasing the soft, gentle, potentially romantic effect of the lighting, Blanche also lights a small candle. Hence the sudden 'headlight of the locomotive' is made more striking and shocking against such a visually muted background. Completely out of keeping with the rest of the scene, this a strong, penetrative light, like a spot-light or the light used for an interrogation. The stage direction informs us that it 'glares' into the room for a moment before passing. This sudden, threatening illumination floods the stage just as Blanche is revealing what happened to her young husband.

Gently fading light features again features at the start of Scene 8. Again, the stage directions describe the light through the flat windows 'fading gradually'. Williams also emphasises that this light is reflected in the urban landscape outside of the flat. It 'blazes on the side of a big water-tank or oil-drum' and the nearby business district becomes 'pierced by pinpoints of lighted windows or windows reflecting the sunset'. The meaning of all this light is ambiguous. While the symbolism of fading light implies something elegiac, a sign of loss of hope and good things coming to an end, the fact that here it fades into a 'still-golden dusk' perhaps holds open the possibility of a more hopeful conclusion to the play's action. On the other hand, the verb 'blazes' implies something violent and short-lived, like sudden anger, while 'pierced' also carries implications both of violence as well as of revelation. The scene that unfolds, of course, is the one of illumination, as Stanley reveals Blanche's unfortunate recent past to her sister. Once again, at the end of the scene, when Blanche is left along on-stage, whispering the words of a song to her, the 'light slowly fades' on her solitary figure.

The threat of exposure to stark, penetrative light is realised finally in Scene 9. Having arrived late in the evening to find Blanche alone in the flat, Mitch 'tears the paper lantern off the light-bulb' and, despite Blanche's desperate protestations, 'turns the light on and stares at her'. Only once he's taken a good long look at her face, does Mitch turn the light off again, returning the flat's lighting to its habitual hazy dimness.

In Scene 10, lighting is used expressionistically to convey Blanche's worst fears. When she warns Stanley not to come into the bedroom, 'lurid reflections

 appear on the walls around Blanche', as if trapping her. The effect is nightmarish as 'the shadows are of a grotesque and menacing form'. This lighting effect is repeated when Blanche tries desperately to ring for help, only this time it is even more dangerous and threatening: the 'shadows and lurid reflections' now move 'sinuously as a flame along the wall spaces', expressing her escalating terror. It's important here that the audience sees what Blanche thinks she sees, that we share her perceptions, as it encourages us to empathise with her.

With a strikingly cinematic lighting effect, at this point, the back wall, becomes 'transparent', so that the audience can witness an unsavoury street scene of robbery, involving a prostitute, a drunkard, a policeman and the negro woman.

The lighting in Scene 11 for the second poker game is the same as for the first game, 'raw' and 'lurid'. However, the light outside is 'turquoise', a colour which carries connotations of spirituality and tranquillity. When Blanche appears from the bathroom, she is framed by a gentle, soft 'amber light' and she seems to emit almost holy 'tragic radiance'. Nevertheless, when Stanley confronts her, the 'lurid reflections' spring up for a third time with their 'sinuous shapes', recalling the terror of the rape scene. Only when the doctor removes his hat and speaks to Blanche in a 'gentle and reassuring' manner do the 'lurid reflections fade'.

Williams uses lighting like a painter or poet, creating strongly visual stage pictures. The lighting ranges from a hazy dimness of the apartment to bright, penetrative spotlight of the locomotive. In between these extremes, the lighting is various shades of blue, including turquoise, and sometimes it is an unnatural looking, potentially queasy looking green. Only once it is a soft amber colour. A distinct feature of Williams' poetic stagecraft is how the lighting not only generates atmosphere, but also works symbolically to convey a character's state of mind.

Soundtrack

As you will be aware from film-tracks, music can convey mood and atmosphere very efficiently and stir the audience's emotions. Watch any exciting chase scene in a film with the sound turned off and the level of excitement will be severely diminished. Music can also be used to convey character and a character's state of mind. A recurring pattern of music, the marshal leitmotif in *Star Wars*, for instance, follows Darth Vader throughout these films. In *Streetcar...*, there are two major musical motifs, the 'blue piano' music of New Orleans and the Varsouviana, polka music Blanche hears when she thinks of the death of her young husband.

We have already noted how the 'blue piano' motif expresses the spirit of New Orleans. Its notes linger in the background during the first scene of the play. As if expressing Stella's unspoken anger, noticeably the blue piano music 'grows louder' at the key moment when Blanche admits to her sister that their childhood home, Belle Reve has been lost. If the blue piano music is associated with Stanley, Stella and where they live, a very different type of music is associated with Blanche. In the final moments of the Scene 1, before Blanche is nearly sick, this new music is heard for the first time. The music of the polka 'rises up' when Stanley questions Blanche about her marriage, connecting these two things, marriage and the polka, in the audience's mind. The fact that the polka music can only be heard faintly 'in the distance' suggests that the traumatic thoughts and feelings associated with her marriage and the death of the 'boy' remain partially buried. If the music grows louder, therefore, this would symbolise the memories becoming stronger and more pressing. The cultural gulf between Blanche and the rest of the characters is neatly conveyed via these motifs. Stella and Stanley's music accords with their surroundings and emanates from the New Orleans streets; Blanche's polka music is classical and refined and was imported originally from European culture.

Another way Williams signals Blanche's highly strung, shaky and nervous state is via sound effects. The sound effect of a cat screeching, for instance, is used several times in Scene 1. Each time she hears it she is disproportionately agitated by it. The first time, when she is alone in the flat, she has to catch 'her breath' afterwards 'with a startled gesture'. At the end of the scene, hearing the cat, 'Blanche springs up', as if ready to run. In both cases, the screech seems to externalise Blanche's jangled sensibility.

The absence of noise can also be used powerfully, such as in the play's first scene. Awkward, uncomfortable silences open up between characters from time to time, and when these happen, quickly they try to speak to cover up their unease. This happens several times in the first exchange between Stella and Blanche, most notably the 'embarrassed silence' when they discuss the small size of the flat and then again when Blanche confesses to having lost Belle Reve. Another awkward silence opens up at the end of Scene 1 when Blanche fails to return Stanley's grin. Whereas both women are flustered by the silences, Stanley calmly begins talking again, as if silence is another weapon in his armoury.

The blue piano music comes into Scene 2 when Stanley enters, connecting it again to him. Again, it lingers in the background, 'perpetual', during the action, only becoming louder this time when Stanley reveals that Stella is pregnant and again, minutes later, when Blanche and Stella leave the stage and the scene ends. This second increase in volume follows two references to the sound effect of off-stage laughter - Blanche's 'desperate laughter' followed immediately by a more powerful 'bellowing laugh' from the men

preparing to play the poker game inside the flat. The men, this implies, will have the last laugh. Moreover, a new element is added to the blue piano music, the 'hot trumpet'. Obviously two instruments coming together suggests two people coming together. Meanwhile, the 'hot' nature of the trumpet echoes the street vendor's cry of 'red hots!' that had so alarmed Blanche and recalls the 'red robe' she wore at the start of the scene. Heat, of course, creates pressure and implies passion.

Scene 3 features several sound effects and pieces of music. The scene starts with silence, which both communicates the players' concentration on their game and allows the audience to take in the striking opening tableaux. A little later we hear a chair scraping and then the 'loud whack' of Stanley slapping Stella on her thigh, followed by the men's laughter. Later again, we hear a 'blow' when Stanley hits Stella, followed by her voice crying out in pain. As the men grapple in the kitchen, something is overturned and there is 'crash'. More off-stage action is indicated when the men manage to wrestle Stanley into the bathroom. From there we hear more 'blows' and then the sound of water running from the shower. At the end of the scene, we hear Eunice dismissively slamming her door on Stanley. Importantly, all the whacks and blows dished out so far in the play happen off-stage, out of our sight.

Whereas in the previous scenes the blue piano has been playing in the background, it is not present here, making the sudden music coming from the bedroom radio seem more pronounced. The colourful music that emerges, exotic 'rhumba' dance music, corresponds to the visual vividness of this scene. When Blanche turns the radio on a second time, the stage directions indicate a specific piece of classical waltz, 'Wein, Wein, nur dul allein'. In the silence following the men forcing Stanley into the bathroom and then making their sharp exit from the flat, we hear music from a 'bar around the corner'. The song is 'Paper Doll' and it's played 'slow and blue'. When Stanley tries and fails to speak to Stella over the phone, suddenly 'dissonant brass and piano sounds' break out and straight afterwards the 'blue piano' plays, but only for a 'brief interval', as if trying, and failing, to reassert itself as the dominant motif of the scene. Stanley's 'heaven-splitting' cry of 'STELL-AHHHHH!' is followed by a new instrument, a 'low-tone clarinet', whose noise is described as 'moans' and, like 'Paper Doll', symbolises Stanley's anguish. The clarinet music 'fades away' once Stella and Stanley leave the scene, cementing the idea of their reconciliation. Hence the final conversation between Blanche and Mitch has no soundtrack.

Scene 3 is a chaotic, violent, bitty, broken-up sort of scene, in which the tone swings rapidly from one extreme to another. There's shouting and silence, dressing up and undressing, physical grappling and physical touching, anger and despair, supplemented by lots of exits and entrances and shifts in the dramatic focus. Alongside the dialogue, stage action, costume and lighting, the sound effects and the short blasts of a wide range of different types of music add greatly to the lurid, overheated and unpredictable effect.

Scene 4 begins with a 'confusion of street cries like a choral chant'. During the rest of the scene, however, the conversation between Stella and Blanche is accompanied by background silence. This is interrupted twice by the sound of a train approaching and passing. As the scene ends with a lingering stage image of Stella and Stanley embracing, the music of the 'blue piano' returns, this time accompanied by a trumpet and also, for the first time, drums. Certainly, drums add dynamism and energy to the music and perhaps also suggest something more ominous.

Sound effects are used several times in Scene 5, often to convey off-stage action. While the audience witness Stella and Blanche's conversation, they hear 'a disturbance' from the flat upstairs. This soon escalates when there is a 'clatter or aluminium striking a wall', a man's 'angry roar', 'overturned furniture' followed by a 'crash'. The domestic violence and possible marital infidelity are, however, presented comically - one of the comic elements some critics have identified in the first half of the play. Far more ominous is the 'murmur of thunder' that follows a little later, signalling the storm that is brewing.

When Stanley, Stella, Steven and Eunice come together and head off for some fun, they are accompanied by the sound of 'trumpet and drums', echoing their excitement and vibrant energy. In contrast, left alone in the flat waiting for Mitch, Blanche is accompanied by 'the music from the Four Deuces' bar, which is 'slow and blue'. Again, here the music expresses the character's mood. This music shifts back into the 'blue piano', starting up as Blanche flirts with the young man and 'continues through the rest of this scene and the opening of the next'.

This music fades away as Blanche and Mitch enter the flat in Scene 6. The lack of background music helps emphasise the awkwardness of the scene. There are several references to nervous coughs, pauses and silences that creep into Blanche and Mitch's conversation. In particular a drawn out, 'considerable silence' followed by Mitch's self-conscious cough, lingers after he has lifted Blanche in the air, and they don't know what else to say to each other.

The pervasive quietness also amplifies the suddenly loud noise of the locomotive as it 'thunders past'. This is followed by the return of the polka music associated with Blanche's past traumas. It starts up at the key moment in Blanche's story, just before Allan shot himself. The fact that it stops 'abruptly' after Blanche says the word 'shot' signals that it is the external expression of her feelings. The polka music starts up again, almost immediately, when Blanche continues the story, but changes from being 'faint with distance' and in a 'minor key' to a stronger 'major key'. The volume of the music increases as Blanche becomes so lost in her memories of that tragic night that, for some moments, she forgets she is in the flat with Mitch. Thus the polka theme conveys the power of this trauma to overwhelm Blanche and destabilise the balance of her mind. Not until Mitch's insistent kisses bring her back to reality does the polka music finally fade out.

In Scene 7, as Stanley dishes the dirt he has uncovered about Blanche and her life in Laurel, intermittently from off-stage can be heard the sound of Blanche singing to herself, laughing and splashing about as she bathes. Obviously, Blanche is unaware of the nature of the conversation and her sweet, happy, care-free singing forms an ironic background to the bitter revelations on stage. The song Williams has chosen for her is also ironic – 'a saccharine popular ballad' about romantic deception leading to love. Poignantly, the repeated chorus line of 'But it wouldn't be make-believe if you believed in me' suggests Blanche's hope that Mitch's feelings for her will have the power to transform fantasy into reality. Meanwhile, the slamming of the bathroom door expresses the ever-increasing tension between Blanche and Stanley. Once again, Williams uses music to express Blanche's disturbed state of mind. As the scene concludes and Blanche realises that something is wrong, the 'distant piano music goes into a hectic breakdown'.

The birthday party in Scene 8 has only been going for less than a page before there is a stage direction saying that the 'music fades out'. Williams hasn't, however, specified which piece of music this is, so directors will have to decide. One option is it to be a continuation of the 'distant piano', in which case, it would indicate how Blanche remains troubled by the new, uncertain atmosphere opening up between herself and Stella, even when they are trying hard to be jolly for her birthday.

When the characters leave the flat, the sound of 'the Negro entertainers around the corner' can be heard, presumably also playing the 'blue piano' motif. There is a later reference to a piano fading out, which seems to confirm this supposition. Again, the ensuing quietness helps accentuate a sound effect, this time the phone ringing. As elsewhere, violent sounds, such as the crash of the crockery Stanley smashes, foreshadow the physical violence to come.

The second major musical motif, the polka music of the 'Varsouviana', 'steals in softy' when Stanley hands Blanche the birthday envelope with the bus ticket back to Laurel inside. Whereas before this music came and went again, now it lingers, underscoring the rest of the scene. Alongside this, the increasingly disturbed state of Blanche is conveyed through the off-stage sounds of her 'coughing' and 'gagging', as she struggles to process what is happening to her. When Stanley and Stella leave to go to the hospital and Blanche emerges from her refuge in the bathroom, the polka music grows ominously louder and faster, 'rising with a sinister rapidity' signalling its increasing hold over Blanche's mind. Moreover, the increased prevalence and intensity of the music suggests that momentum is now building inexorably towards a psychological crisis.

This music continues in Scene 9, its ominous effect shown by the way Blanche is now drinking 'to escape it and the sense of disaster closing in on her'. It stops, momentarily, when Blanche hears the doorbell and realises it is Mitch, only to start up again as she realises his visit isn't of a romantic nature. As he was before in Scene 6, Mitch is unable to hear the music, enhancing the audience's impression that, unlike the blue piano, the polka music is a figment only of Blanche's imagination and conveys the stage of her mind. This impression is re-enforced by the fact that Blanche 'touches her forehead' before the music starts up again. Again, there is the sound of a shot. As Blanche notes, the music 'always stop after that', except that this time the music lingers afterwards, and, indeed, returns for a third time in the scene after the entrance of the Mexican woman. Finally it fades away when Blanche's thoughts are forced out of past troubles and into the present ones when Mitch seizes her around the waist. Once Mitch has gone and a forlorn Blanche is left alone on stage, we hear the 'distant piano' again 'slow and blue', suitably melancholy.

When Stanley enters Scene 10, he is accompanied by the soundtrack of the 'honky-tonk music', his slightly inebriated state signalled by his whistling. Later, with typical physical gusto, he opens a beer-bottle by 'pounding' it on the corner of a table. Things escalate with Blanche's failed phone call to Shep.

 Suddenly the night is 'filled with inhuman voices like cries in a jungle', expressing her growing terror and anticipating the primitive brutality to come. The 'clicking' of the phone after Blanche has put it down makes a 'steady' and 'rasping' sound that betrays her actions to Stanley. As Stanley and Blanche face off, the blue piano music rises, beginning to 'drum up louder' until the music morphs into the 'roar of an approaching locomotive' and back again. The sense of Blanche's confusion and fear is conveyed sonically through the harsh mishmash of sounds, as alongside the piano, now the inhuman jungle voices also 'rise up', as things move towards their crisis. Two crashes follow in quick succession: First the bottle Blanche smashes, and the table is overturned when Stanley 'springs towards her'. When Stanley overpowers Blanche and carries her inert body to the bed, we hear the 'hot trumpet and drums' sounding 'loudly' as if celebrating his triumph over her.

Scene 11 opens with the cleansing sound of water running from the bathroom, where Blanche is washing herself again. Despite her attempts to wash away the past, when she enters, she is accompanied again by the haunting music of the 'Varousvianna'. Whereas the background sounds from the streets of New Orleans have been dominated previously by the music of the blue piano, now we hear for the first time 'cathedral bells' chiming, a sound Blanche herself describes, tellingly, as the 'only clean thing in the Quarter'. As Blanche delivers a monologue about dying at sea, these chimes accompany her words twice more, emphasising their symbolic importance. However, the possibility of spiritual redemption and purification the bells signal is countered by the sounds of what is happening inside the flat. There is the constant background of the men playing their game of poker and then the doorbell.

Blanche's increasing anxiety about the nature of this caller is signalled again by the 'Varsouvianna' music starting up again, faintly, in the background, this time accompanied by drums. It stops for at the moment when Blanche realises that her visitor is not Shep Huntleigh and Stella and her stare at each other. The short silence, with only the sound of Stanley 'steadily shuffling the cards', creates a pregnant pause. And then Blanche tries to flee, only to be blocked off by Stanley, at which point the trauma of her past and of her recent rape merge and the 'Varsouvianna' distorts weirdly, 'accompanied by the cries and noise of the jungle'. Blanche's frenzied, possibly crazed, state is then emphasised by echoing voices, as if we are inside her head. The cacophony only dies out, when the doctor manages to calm Blanche and lead her away. The soundtrack of the play ends with the sound of Stella's 'luxurious sobbing', underscored by the swelling music of the 'blue piano' and, as Stanley tries to comfort his wife, with the 'muted trumpet'.

So, as well as the two dominant musical motifs, there are various other bits of music used in the play, drawing on a wide range of musical styles. There's a classical waltz, a popular song, a rhumba. Alongside side the music, the play's soundtrack also features many different sound effects, from the cat's screeching in Scene 1 to the cathedral bells in scene 11. Sometimes different music is played in quick succession, creating a confused, almost dissonant effect, and a few times music and sound effects merge to more disturbing effect, most notably, the jungle voices and the polka in Scene 11. Sometimes too, the absence or quietness of sound, particularly after loudness, can be dramatically powerful. The moment, for instance, when Blanche first sees the doctor in Scene 11, slowly realises what is happening, and stares at her sister and Stella stares back at her, is made more powerful by the 'moment of silence' between them. A moment when other outcomes might just be possible; a silence and stillness during which the audience is sucked into imagining what might be going on inside the heads of the two characters. A silent communion between the sisters, accompanied only by the sound of Stanley 'steadily shuffling the cards', as if he is the master of their fates

Costumes

Tellingly, when the two women are first introduced to us, we are not informed what Stella is wearing, whereas **Blanche's** striking manner of dress is emphasised in detail. We have already seen Stanley and Mitch, dressed in denim work clothes, and they seem a natural fit for a grubby, slightly edgy, urban context. Blanche, however, looks entirely out of place; 'her appearance is incongruous to this setting'. In contrast to the men's characteristic roughness, she is 'daintily dressed' in a 'white suit with fluffy bodice, necklace and ear-rings of pearl, white gloves and a hat'. She looks 'as if she were arriving at a summer tea or cocktail party in the garden district'. The insistent whiteness of the outfit, of  course, attempts to signal virginal purity, while the pearl jewellery suggests ostentatious wealth, class consciousness and luxury. Her delicacy and vulnerability, particularly in this context, are also emphasised by the comparison to a 'moth', an image which also foreshadows her self-destructive qualities.

At the start of Scene 2, Blanche's clothing is again emphasised in contrast to her sister's, signalling its greater significance in terms of Blanche's sense of self and her projection of her identity to others. Indicating the trouble ahead, Blanche's dress with its feminine 'flower print' has been 'laid out on Stella's bed'. When Blanche leaves the bathroom to find Stanley waiting to confront her, she is dressed only in a 'red satin robe'. This sexually provocative outfit projects a very different image to her initial appearance in delicate whites. Red has obvious connotations of passion and sex, and these qualities are complemented by the tactile attractiveness of satin. A sinuous fabric, such as satin, is also likely to be figure hugging. Alongside her flirtatious behaviour in this scene, the signals this robe gives off prompt Stanley into forming new ideas about what kind of woman Blanche really is. Separated from Stanley only by a pair of drapes, Blanche then changes into her 'flowered print dress' and asks Stanley to button it up at the back for her.

Later, in Scene 3, Blanche takes off her blouse to reveal a pink bra she is wearing underneath. Although she is in a different room to the men, Blanche is well-aware that she can be seen through the chinks of light of the curtain. Standing on purpose in this light, moments later she makes no attempt to cover up her semi-nakedness when an infuriated Stanley stomps into the bedroom. In marked contrast, Stella goes to the private space of the bathroom to change. While Stella changes off-stage into to a demure 'light blue kimono', on-stage Blanche slips into her 'dark red satin wrapper'.

The development of Blanche's character is expressed visually by her changes in clothes. A small, but significant shift in what these clothes express is revealed in the stage directions in Scene 9. Here Williams describes the same red, satin robe for the first time as being 'scarlet'. A 'scarlet woman' is a pejorative term for a woman infamous for her promiscuity: hence the colour 'scarlet' associates Blanche with prostitutes and, ultimately, with the figure of the Whore of Babylon. And, of course, Blanche wears this robe during the scene where she reveals the most sordid elements of her past to Mitch.

At the start of Scene 10, a partially drunk Blanche has 'decked herself out in a somewhat soiled and crumpled white satin evening gown and a pair of scuffed silvers slippers' and has placed the 'rhinestone tiara' on her head. Of course, the outfit recalls the dainty white one she wore when she arrived at Elysian Fields just a few months ago, and the changes are striking. The fact that the dress is 'soiled' and 'crumpled' and the shoes 'scuffed' symbolises the damage that has been done to Blanche's reputation and reflects how her façade of gentility and sophistication is no longer able to hide her disreputable past. The fact that she has dressed herself in this fantastic get-up signals her inability to face reality.

Blanche's final costume change expresses her desire for purification and redemption for the sins of her past. As Scene 11 opens, Blanche is dressed again in her red satin robe and its sensual and sexual associations are emphasised in the stage directions through the comment on her this sinuous material cleaves to the 'sculptured lines of her body'. When she gets ready to greet her visitor, Blanche changes into a dress and puts on a jacket that is 'Della Robbia blue. The blue of the robe in the old Madonna pictures'. Williams implies that it is not just Blanche's wish, but that she has indeed been redeemed, in the Catholic sense of being absolved through her suffering, like a martyr, as even in her red robe Blanche now emits a 'tragic radiance'.

It's not just the actor playing Blanche who has to strip off and reveal flesh in various scenes. The stage directions include several different outfits for **Stanley**, and we see him frequently changing from one to another on-stage, often blithely ignoring Blanche's presence as he does so.

Stage directions inform us that at the start of the play Stanley and Mitch are both 'roughly dressed in blue denim work clothes'. [Denim in this period hadn't yet become fashionable, so this costume reflects the common, manual work wear of ordinary working men.] Stanley also carries his bowling jacket, suggesting masculine sports. At the end of the first scene, when he is alone in the flat with a sister-in-law who he has just met, Stanley removes his shirt to reveal his bare torso. While this could be considered as an example simply of his uncouthness, it seems more calculated - a deliberately provocative move in the sexually charged power game Stanley is already playing with Blanche.

In Scene 5, Stanley again undresses and dresses on stage, removing his vibrant 'green and scarlet silk bowling shirt', changing to be ready to go out with Stella. A clue that he is smartening himself up to go out is the fact that he puts on a tie. Stanley takes off some clothes again in Scene 8, this time 'ripping off his shirt' to change into his 'brilliant silk bowling shirt' to go off and play sport with his buddies. He removes his shirt again in front of Blanche when they are alone in the flat in Scene 10. Memorably, in the aftermath of the drunken poker game in Scene 3, after the men have rough-handled Stanley into the shower to try and sober him up, he emerges from the bathroom, 'dripping water and still in his clinging wet polka dot drawers'. Clinging. So, basically, he's wet and all-but naked and he remains in a similar state until the end of the scene.

Filming, of course, brings with it the capacity for close-ups and long, lingering shots. Unsurprisingly, as the play was written and first performed in the late 1940s, when it was first filmed in 1951, some of its steamier, more sexually charged moments fell foul of the official censors. Commenting on how film versions brought out the sexuality of Williams' plays, R. Barton Palmer notes perceptively that the playwright's male characters are 'less the bearers of sexual desire – the traditional male role in American theatre and film – and more its object, thereby assuming what is conventionally a female position. Such femininization,' he continues, 'is homoerotic to some degree, but it creates an appeal from which female viewers are by no means immune,' especially in plays where the female characters are given the 'traditional male role of desiring subject'[8]. Certainly, Marlon Brando's 'sizzling incarnation' with his 'raw physical magnetism' fits Palmer's description.

Even when he is absent from scenes, Stanley's presence is felt. Although he is absent from the start of Scene 4, for instance, Stanley's 'gaudy pyjamas lie across the threshold of the bathroom', as if marking his territory. The bathroom, of course, is the place Blanche claims as her sanctuary. When he does enter Scene 4, Stanley is wearing an 'undershirt and grease-stained seersucker pants', an outfit that, like the earlier denim, emphasises his working-class credentials.

Clothes maketh the man, or so they say. Stanley's bright, confident, colourful costumes are an outward expression of his role of 'gaudy seed-bearer'. Unlike Blanche, who is haunted by corruption and death, as a 'seed-bearer' Stanley is a vigorous progenitor of life. As the stage directions in Scene 1 also establish, he presents himself like a 'richly feathered male bird among hens'. The hypocrisy of a culture that condemned female sexuality while valorising male sexual potency and promiscuity is subtly suggested by the fact that the same colour, 'scarlet', is worn by both Stanley and Blanche. However, for Stanley the colour expresses vitality without carrying the negative connotations that tarnish Blanche.

Once again, Stanley's costume and his dressing and undressing are prominent features in Scene 10. Initially, he is wearing his 'vivid green silk bowling shirt', but within minutes of entering the flat, where he finds an anxious and

---

[8] R. Barton Palmer, Hollywood in Crisis, *The Cambridge Companion to Tennessee Williams*.

inebriated Blanche alone, he starts unbuttoning and then removing his shirt in front of her. The sexual violence to come is prefigured by Stanley taking out and examining the brilliantly coloured silk pyjamas he wore on his wedding night and that we saw earlier. When minutes later a panicked Blanche tries to ring for help, Stanley throws open the bathroom door and emerges in these 'brilliant silk pyjamas', with a 'tasselled sash' knotted at the waist.

Mitch's duller, more stolid nature is reflected in how he is dressed and also by how he is reluctant to undress. In particular, in the intimate Scene 6, when he is alone in the flat late at night with Blanche, Mitch keeps on his woollen over-coat. The play is set in the summer, and we know from various comments by various characters that the weather is very warm, so Mitch's wool over-coat seems inappropriately heavy. Whereas Stanley seems to divest himself of clothes at the drop of a hat, expressing both his dominance and freedom from restraint, and Blanche does so for calculated seductive effect, even when he enters the bedroom, Mitch has to be cajoled into even loosening his stiff collar and then into taking this coat off. In part, Mitch's awkwardness here is because, like 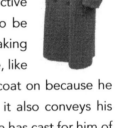 Blanche, he also has something to hide – he keeps his coat on because he doesn't want to reveal how much he is sweating – but it also conveys his general clumsy ill-ease and his poor fit for the role Blanche has cast for him of dashing cavalier.

Having not shown up for Blanche's birthday party, later the same evening, Mitch arrives at the flat, worse for wear. This time he doesn't bother to dress up at all, arriving in his everyday denim work clothes. The costume indicates he no longer feels he needs to impress Blanche and that he's ready to get down to brass tacks.

And what of **Stella**, the other principal character? What do we learn about her costumes? Not much. There are a few specific details, such as the 'light blue satin kimono' she dons in Scene 3, but generally what Stella is wearing doesn't seem to have been very important for the playwright. Nor does the actor playing Stella have to undress on-stage in front of other characters, unlike those playing both Blanche and Stanley. Perhaps Stella's natural beauty is enough to distinguish her from the crowd or perhaps the lack of detail about her costume indicates the way she can seem to blend and fade into the background, particularly in the presence of the brighter more colourful characters of her husband and sister.

The costumes of the other men are important because they show they are members of the same tribe. This is most obvious from the fact that they wear the same work clothes and dress up in similar leisurewear, such as the bright coloured shirts for the poker game.

When the doctor and matron enter in the play's final scene, they emanate the 'gravity of their profession' and have the 'unmistakable aura of the state institution'. Although Williams doesn't specify exactly what they are wearing, it is easy for the reader, and a director, to imagine costumes that would create this aura. We do learn that the matron is wearing a 'severe dress' and the doctor must be wearing a hat, as he takes this off at a crucial moment and changes the atmosphere of the scene.

Props

Props can also be used as emblems of character. In Shakespeare's plays, for instance, the heroes invariably brandish and use swords, whereas the Machiavellian villains, such as Iago, Claudius and Goneril, use poison. Similarly, in *Streetcar...* the objects associated with the various characters reveal important information about their personalities.

Before reading the next section, see how many props you can re-call from just Scene 1 of *Streetcar....* Once you've listed these, consider their function. What would the play lose if these props were deleted?

Here's our list:

1. The red-stained package from the butcher's
2. Blanche's valise
3. Blanche's slip of paper
4. Blanche's purse
5. The whiskey bottle and the half-opened closet. [Some stage items, such as this closet and the chair, can either be considered part of the state set or as props]
6. The glass
7. Blanche's cigarette
8. Blanche's handkerchief
9. The photograph of Stanley.

The audience's attention is drawn to the packet due to its bright red colour and unknown contents, by the fact that Stanley 'heaves' it at Stella who just about manages to catch it and the question about it asked by the negro woman. We soon learn that it contains 'meat', though of what type doesn't seem important because, obviously, Stanley bringing the meat home signals that he is the apex hunter. Mitch doesn't carry a similar packet, suggesting he might not be able to bring the meat home.

What is the difference between a suitcase and a valise? Not much in practical terms. A valise is just a small suitcase. And, in any case, an audience watching the play won't know that Williams described Blanche carrying a valise.

Nevertheless, with its French origins, the word 'valise' carries connotations of sophistication and style that the words 'small suitcase' do not, a hint to the costume designer about the nature of this prop. Its smallness is also significant, implying that either Blanche doesn't intend to stay for long or that she has been reduced to few possessions. Or both. Later, however a large 'wardrobe trunk' appears in the flat, containing armfuls of dresses and other dressing up costumes.

When she first goes into the flat, Blanche is described as sitting stiffly on a chair with her 'hands tightly clutching her purse as if she were quite cold'. This clutching conveys her nervous anxiety, but also, suggests she doesn't feel safe in this alien, urban environment. Obviously, Blanche's grabbing the bottle and necking of 'half a tumbler of whisky' quickly establishes her drink problem and this impression is confirmed by the way her glass shakes violently the second time she has a drink. Additionally, she helps herself to somebody else's property – the drink it turns out is Stanley's – and also shamelessly lies about it first to Stella and then later to a sceptical Stanley. Meanwhile, Stanley's close examination of the whisky bottle shows how quickly he is on to Blanche's deceptions.

Both the way Blanche handles the cigarette - 'nervously tamping' it - and dabs at her forehead with her handkerchief indicate her state of high-strung agitation, verging on nervous hysteria.

The photograph of Stanley reveals his wife's pride in him, particularly in his handsome appearance, and fills in a bit of his backstory, informing us that Stanley not only served in the army in WWII, but that he took on a leadership role as a 'master sergeant' and that he was awarded medals for his service.

In Scene 2, a few more props appear in the play:
1. Blanche's trunk
2. The clothes within it, including expensive looking 'fox fur-pieces'
3. The 'fistful' of jewellery, including bracelets and a tiara

4. Stanley's cigarette
5. Blanche's atomizer
6. Blanche's tin box
7. Various sheafs of paper, including legal documents and the love letters tied with a ribbon, and a large envelope containing more papers
8. Blanche's glasses, which could also be classified as costume
9. The carton of drink Stella brings back form the drug-store
10. A case of beer carried by Steve and Pablo.

The appearance of Blanche's trunk belies the impression she gave in Scene 1 that she was only intending to make a short visit. Additionally, it gives Blanche a theatrical air, as if she is an actress with lots of dressing up costumes. We also first see the trunk right slap bang in the middle of the Kowalski's bedroom, invading their private space, a space we know is limited in a cramped flat. Meanwhile, Stanley's total lack of respect for Blanche's property, mirroring hers for his, is shown by the way he pulls the trunk open when she in the bathroom, without her permission to do so and despite Stella's protest. He then rifles through the contents before he 'jerks out an armful of dresses' and then 'jerks open' a drawer and pulls out a 'fistful of costume jewellery'.

The contents of the trunk tell us more about Blanche – it contains not only her actual but also her emotional baggage. At the same time, his reaction to these contents tells us more about Stanley. That Blanche has furs and jewellery, albeit possibly inexpensive furs and fake, costume jewellery, suggests she has been living a very different, more exotic, more upper-class social life than the

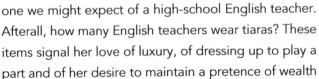

one we might expect of a high-school English teacher. Afterall, how many English teachers wear tiaras? These items signal her love of luxury, of dressing up to play a part and of her desire to maintain a pretence of wealth and sophistication. It may only be costume jewellery, like that word by an actor in a play, but it is convincing enough to fool someone like Stanley. Enraged, he pulls out what he thinks are 'pearls' and 'diamonds', 'gold bracelets' and a 'crown for an empress'.

As Stanley observes, these items signal how Blanche comes from an entirely different world to the proletarian Kowalskis, a genteel, aristocratic world of privilege and wealth. When he demands 'where are your pearls and diamonds?' he is making a political point about the unjust distribution of wealth in the old America. Stella has to calm him down and correct the false impression he has formed. That 'crown for an empress' is just a tiara made out of 'rhinestone'. However, even if they are fake, for Stanley these regal-seeming items are also symbols of the threat Blanche to poses to his dominant position as the 'king' of his home: Blanche has moved into his home, taken the attention of his wife and conducts herself with the airs and graces of a Queen. The rough way he handles these items expresses his fury at this situation.

Of all the items in the trunk, one has the most value for Blanche – her tin box which contains her love letters from Allan Grey. Again, Stanley shows no regard for Blanche's feelings or her privacy, snatching them and starting to read them. The violence of Blanche's response when she snatches them back reveals how important this relationship still is for her. To her, Stanley even touching the letters feels like an intrusion.

She is more willing to share the other letters with him, the legal correspondence about Belle Reve. After putting on glasses to peruse them, a detail that hints that she is older than she pretends, Blanche hands 'Stanley the entire box'. In fact, Blanche seems almost relieved to hand these papers over, as if there is something a bit grubby and unladylike about business concerns. For some critics, the moment in which these documents are passed from Blanche to Stanley signals the passing of power from the old culture to the new America and/or from aristocratic power to more democratic forces.

Scene 3:
1. Slices of watermelon
2. Whisky bottles and glasses
3. The towel
4. The small white radio

5. Mitch's silver cigarette case
6. The Lucky cigarettes and matches
7. Blanche's little coloured paper lantern
8. The telephone.

Many scenes in the play include a bottle of whisky and at least one character drinking heavily, fuelling the sense of excess, transgression and potential danger. This time, of course, it is Stanley who gets drunk, a process that releases his pent-up anger and realises his potential for violence.

The towel is another important prop. Distracted by the sudden appearance of Blanche in the flat, Mitch absent-mindedly carries it out of the bathroom with him. When he realises he still has it in his hands, he laughs a little with embarrassment. Alongside his shy cough, his being embarrassed is enough to convince Blanche that he might have a more sensitive nature than his peers. Mitch's action also show the immediately powerful effect Blanche has on him.

Blanche plays a European waltz on the little white radio. Drunk and infuriated by the various disruptions to his poker game in the kitchen, Stanley enters the bedroom 'fiercely', 'snatches' the radio off the table and, swearing, hurls it out of the window. Perhaps any sort of music might have triggered this violent reaction, but the fact that the music is a classical piece and Blanche is waltzing to it, as if she is at a glittery Southern ball, has led some critics to argue that Stanley's actions symbolise a wider violent rejection of a supposedly superior culture by the new urban class he represents. Elsewhere in the play, Blanche tries and fails to convince her sister of the worth of 'art, and poetry and music' and she tells Mitch that her students no longer seem to care about 'Hawthorne and Whitman and Poe'. In this reading, throwing the radio out of the window, Stanley tries to rid his home a higher culture that for too long has looked down its nose at the likes of him. And in this sense, it foreshadows his eventual violence and eviction of the embodiment of those superior values, Blanche.

The short scene that plays out as Mitch shows Blanche the inscription of his cigarette is brilliantly concentrated. On the one hand, we see Mitch trying to impress Blanche with something pretty in his possession. On the other, we see her gently manipulating him, pretending not to be able to read the inscription so that Mitch will have to move closer to her and strike a match. From Mitch's point of view, Blanche's immediate recognition of the lines of poetry confirms his impression of her cultural sophistication. From her point of view, carrying such an object confirms her feelings that Mitch is a little superior to his peers and has the potential to be a chivalrous rescuer.

Although it already seems that Mitch might be smitten, Blanche asks him to put the coloured lantern over the light bulb in the bedroom, despite this scene  taking place in Stanley and Stella's bedroom, as the other characters occupy the kitchen. Getting Mitch to perform small, menial tasks for her, Blanche uses the lantern to signal her delicate refinement, telling him that she cannot 'stand a naked light-bulb, any more than I can a rude remark or vulgar action'. Of course, it is easier for Blanche to continue the enchantment of Mitch in a softer, more intimate, less revealing light. Additionally, Mitch's willingness to fit the lantern shows that, unlike Stanley, he is complicit in the creation of Blanche's romantic illusions. Mitch may accuse Blanche of deceiving him later in the play, but we see him here helping to create the deception.

Trace the verbs Williams uses to describe Stanley's habitual ways of interacting with the world around him and you'll find words like 'rips', 'pushes', 'tears', 'snatches', 'hurls', 'smashes', 'jerks' crop up frequently. Frustrated by being separated from Stella, at the end of Scene 3, Stanley 'hurls' the phone on which he's trying to contact her onto the floor. Stanley's appetite for destruction may shock Blanche, who will be its ultimate victim, but it thrills Stella. Like the paper lantern, the phone will be important later in the play when Blanche tries and fails to make calls using it.

Scene 4:
1. A broom Stella twirls in her hands
2. The Kleenex and eyebrow pencil

3. Blanche's purse
4. Various packages carried by Stanley.

It doesn't take long for the relationship between Blanche and Stella to resemble that between a lady and her personal maid. Frequently we see Stella fetching things for her older sister or cooking for her or carrying out small chores, like laying out her clothes for her. When Stella picks up the broom, Blanche commands her to 'Let go of that broom' because she won't allow Stella to clean up after Stanley. Not after *Stanley*. Not unreasonably, Stella asks, well who else is going to do it: 'Then who's going to do it? Are you?' Blanche's response is so shocked and indignant that she can only repeat the same single syllable: 'I? I!'. A lady such as her stoop to do a spot of domestic tidying? Why, the very idea is appalling! Surely to God, that is what one employs servants for. Is Stella losing her mind? The little exchange over the broom tells us a great deal about both sisters. During her long stay at the Kowalskis, true to her word, we never see Blanche pick up a broom or do any domestic chores.

How realistic are Blanche's various attempts to contact Shep Huntleigh? Is he and their relationship just a part of her fantasy world? Or is he, perhaps, a client? The fact that Blanche begins to dash off a letter to him using a piece of Kleenex and an eyebrow pencil implies her plan is not realistic. And she soon gives it up, smashing the pencil on the table in frustration.

Scene 5:
1. A palm leaf
2. The letter Blanche is writing to Shep
3. Some shoes
4. Blanche's bottle of cologne and her handkerchief
5. A bottle of coke
6. Another bottle of whiskey
7. A glass
8. Stanley's drink tucked under his belt
9. Blanche's hand mirror

10. Blanche's long cigarette holder
11. The young man's lighter
12. Mitch's bunch of roses.

As Scene 5 opens we see Blanche seated, fanning herself with a palm leaf, like an Egyptian Queen. The only surprise is that Stella isn't doing the fanning. Repeated references to Blanche trying to cool herself, such as with her dampened handkerchief, also convey her habitually agitated and delicate state of mind as well as the overheated atmosphere of the play, like the heat before a storm breaks. Additionally, Blanche applies a bit of cologne just as Stanley starts honing-in on her past at the Flamingo hotel, as if, unconsciously, she is trying to cover up and protect herself from the bad smell of the past. Three times in a few lines, she dabs at her temples with the handkerchief, a gesture that also signals how she is feeling the pressure of Stanley's scrutiny.

Each time Blanche has to handle a glass during this scene, her hand shakes so badly it almost 'slips from her grasp'. Her increased state of agitation is also communicated by the incident with the coke bottle. When Stella pours it into a glass the coke 'foams over and spills' onto Blanche's 'pretty white skirt' and she 'gives a piercing cry'. The 'piercing' cry seems disproportionate. But, clearly this stage action is symbolically important. Things are indeed slipping from Blanche's grasp, and her white outfit is soiled at the same time her reputation is soiled by Stanley's revelations about her recent past.

Although we see various characters, including Blanche, smoking during the course of the play, this is the only time Williams has Blanche choose to smoke with a 'long holder'. Which prompts the question why? Hard though it might be for modern readers and audiences to believe, but at one time, smoking using a long holder was considered to be elegant and seductive. For those in doubt, google images of the Hollywood actress Audrey Hepburn. Blanche's use of the long holder signals her intentions, and, as she does with Mitch, she asks the young man to light her cigarette for her, so that he has to perform a small act of kindness for her and to bring him physically closer to her.

Scene 6:
1. A plaster statue of the Hollywood actress Mae West
2. Blanche's purse
3. The candle stub and the bottle
4. Two glasses of alcohol.

Naturally, when Mitch and Blanche enter the flat after their not entirely successful date night, Blanche is keen not to turn on the lights and instead lights a candle. This lighting effect helps her in her attempts to conceal her real age from Mitch and to generate an intimate, romantic atmosphere. Through the scene there are a couple of references to Blanche, but not Mitch, drinking quickly.

Scene 7:
1. Birthday cake, candles, flowers and other decorations
2. Towels
3. Stanley's cigarettes
4. Blanche's hairbrush.

It is Stella, of course, who we see setting out the decorations for Blanche's birthday dinner. Meanwhile, Blanche, of course, is once again completing her purification ritual in the bathroom. When she emerges from the bathroom, she asks her sister to fetch her another towel, though the request is couched in the form of an imperative: 'Give me another bath-towel to dry my hair with'. Of course, Stella does so, without complaint.

Though she pretends to ignore Stanley's obvious hostility, speaking breezily to her sister about how refreshed she feels after a hot bath and a cool drink, Blanche's body language tells a different story. She is described as 'snatching up' the hairbrush and then 'brushing her hair vigorously'. The slowing down of her brushing coincides with her realisation that something's wrong.

Scene 8:
1. Knives and forks, cup and sauce, plates etc.

2. A pork chop
3. Stanley's cigarette
4. The phone
5. Cake with candles
6. Tumbler of water
7. The birthday envelope
8. The washcloth.

The way Stanley uses his fork to 'spear his pork chop and how he then eats it with his fingers recalls the first time we saw him in the play in hunter-gatherer mode with the red package of meat. His animalistic way of eating goes against the refined manners expected of a gentleman and leads to Stella calling him a pig. Stanley reacts furiously, hurling a plate to the floor.

Later he gets his revenge when he hands Blanche her birthday present, a little envelope. Blanche is clearly delighted to be given a gift and as she tries to express this, Stanley interrupts her with the bitter truth – it's a ticket back home.

After struggling to process this cruel bit of theatre, Blanche creeps out of the bathroom, at the end of the scene, 'twisting a washcloth', reminding us of her compulsion to make herself clean again.

Scene 9:
1. A bottle of liquor and a glass
2. The mirror
3. Make-up and cologne
4. The electric fan
5. Mitch's cigarette
6. The paper lantern.

After the recent disaster of the birthday party, it is not surprising that Scene 9 opens with Blanche drinking heavily again. Blanche hides the liquor bottle when she hears the doorbell and when she pretends to find it again, Mitch is not fooled or impressed; he just 'stares at her contemptuously'. Noticeably, when he arrived, Mitch lit his own cigarette and didn't offer one to Blanche, where previously they smoked together. His ugly, irritable mood is also indicated by his random hostility to the fan. One of the key moments in the scene, and in the play, is when Mitch insists on seeing Blanche in unadulterated light. He 'tears the paper lantern off the light-bulb', switches the light on and has a long look at Blanche 'good and plain'. This is the moment that Blanche's spell is broken and Mitch is disenchanted.

Scene 10:
1. The wardrobe trunk, tiara and dresses
2. The hand mirror
3. Stanley's beer bottles
4. The telephone
5. The prostitute's sequinned bag
6. The smashed bottle.

The presence of the of trunk in the 'centre of the bedroom' emphasises Blanche's intrusion into Stella and Stanley's life as well as the theatrical nature of the garb she has dressed herself in, as if she is setting off for a glittery ball. Blanche's reluctance to face reality, not least the reality of her own aging, is conveyed by the way that, after looking at herself, she 'slams' the hand mirror with such 'violence that the glass cracks'. The cracking of her own reflection is obviously symbolic and also ominous.

When things start to turn nasty in the flat, Blanche twice tries to use the telephone to call for help and, both times, fails. Her frightened, garbled conversation on the phone to an operator who doesn't understand what she wants is dramatically powerful. Twice she has attempted to ring for help before Stanley enters the scene. Now the same phone betrays her, making a giveaway clicking noise. When Stanley ominously takes his time to 'deliberately' set it 'back on the hook' it confirms his complete control of the situation, as well as Blanche's helplessness and the cutting off of any hope of rescue.

Blanche's last desperate attempt to protect herself with the broken bottle is doomed to fail and seems only to further excite Stanley and perhaps even incite his violence.

Scene 11:
1. The trunk and the flowery dresses
2. The silver-backed mirror
3. The bunch of grapes
4. The poker cards
5. Blanche's paper lantern
6. The baby's pale blue blanket.

Frequently we see Blanche with mirrors, for obvious reasons. That she has a hand mirror and appears to have had this one repaired suggests a continual need to check on how she looks.

At first the bunch of grapes may seem like a pointless or random prop, but they add again to the cosmopolitan picture of New Orleans. Moreover, Blanche's concern for them being washed conveys both her distrust of the salubriousness of her surrounding, and also, more importantly, externalises her own desire for being spiritually cleansed.

When Blanche retreats back into the flat, pursued by the matron, Stanley tears the paper lantern off the light-bulb. The stage direction makes explicit the close connection psychological between this lantern and Blanche herself when Williams writes that as Stanley tears it, she 'cries out as if the lantern was herself'.

Williams could have chosen any colour of blanket for Stella's baby. Pale blue might suggest the baby is male, but is also a colour associated, as we saw with Blanche's 'pretty blue jacket', with purity. The colour symbolism connects the baby to Blanche, not to the garish colours associated with Stanley. And the baby, of course, is a symbol for the hope of a better future in which the conflicts embodied by Blanche and Stanley will be reconciled.

Entrances and exits

When a playwright is restricted in the range of stagecraft he or she can utilise, not only do the devices they employ become more prominent, but other integral aspects of stage business also become more significant.

The play opens with Eunice and 'the negro woman'. Briefly there's a sailor and a street vendor. The characters speak at once, their voices 'overlapping'. Then we see Stanley and Mitch and Stanley throws Stella the bloody packet of meat. Importantly, only Eunice is on stage when Blanche enters and the two of them speak, rather awkwardly, with Eunice trying to make polite chit-chat. Blanche is then left alone for a short period inside the flat. This provides an opportunity to convey her agitated mental state by the way she sits 'tightly clutching her purse' as if she is cold and to reveal her dependence on alcohol. Blanche spies a bottle of whiskey and immediately 'springs up', 'pours half a tumbler' and 'tosses it down'. Of course, Blanche's equally powerful desire to hide her drinking, and the problems associated with this, is also established. Putting the bottle back 'carefully' so it's not obvious it's been moved, she then washes out the glass. Later in the scene she will, of course, deny that she has drunk any of the whiskey, first to her sister and then to a sceptical Stanley.

There follows the first developed conversation, here between Stella and Blanche. Together on stage the sisters can talk more freely than they can when in male company. Significantly Williams has Stella leave, going to the bathroom, so that she is not present during the first meeting of Blanche and Stanley. Stanley's entrance immediately expresses his masculine power and confidence. Vigorously he 'throws open the screen door of the kitchen and comes in'. When he sees her, he eyes Blanche with a calculatingly sexual eye. Blanche cannot help 'drawing back involuntarily from his stare'. The fraught, tense nature of their relationship is immediately established.

At the start of Scene 2, Blanche is in the bathroom, bathing. Her removal from the scene allows Williams to show us Stanley and Stella talking together for the first time. Though Stanley is never bothered about what Blanche hears him say, he can be even more frank with her not around. When Blanche emerges from her bath, Stella goes outside to give her sister some privacy to get changed. Stanley, of course, remains inside the flat. An awkward scene develops as Stanley questions Blanche about Belle Reve while she is changing into her dress. A little later in the scene, Blanche asks Stella to go and fetch her a drink from the drug-store, removing her sister entirely from the scene. Again, we are shown Stanley and Blanche together in the small, cramped space of the apartment, before the scene ends with the two sisters setting off together. The mirroring of the Stanley and Stella interaction with the Stanley and Blanche one is, of course, ominous.

Williams manoeuvres his cast of characters around skilfully in Scene 3, The Poker Night, so that we witness various combinations and clashes. In effect, within the overall scene there's a rapid succession of min-scenes, as the dramatic focus shifts this way and then that, from kitchen to bedroom to bathroom and back again. Initially just the men are assembled on stage, engaging in sports related men talk. Then, briefly, we see Stella and Blanche together, before they enter the bear pit of the poker game. Then we witness how their presence is received by the men. Sending Mitch off to the bathroom facilitates his first chance meeting with Blanche. This short moment is followed by a longer discussion of him by the two sisters. Henceforth, the poker game is intercut with several short episodes where an obviously smitten Mitch sneaks several conversations with Blanche. This fragmentary scene builds to a frantic and violent climax with all the characters present on stage at one time or another, or leaving and then re-entering the stage in quick succession. In a series of very short, choppy mini scenes, it concludes with Stanley alone, then Stanley reunited with Stella before the dramatic attention switches to the blossoming relationship between Blanche and Mitch. As well as exposing the structure within The Poker Night, noticing the switches in dramatic attention also reveals the potential scenes Williams chooses not to show, such as what is happening elsewhere while Blanche and Mitch are politely conversing.

After the mayhem of Scene 3, the pace of Scene 4 is much slower and our dramatic attention more settled. Rather than being broken up into multiple mini scenes with most of the cast on stage, one conversation comprises most of the action, another duologue between the two sisters and most of the scene takes place in one location, the bedroom. Alone, the sisters can talk more freely and, worried about her sister's Blanche seizes the opportunity to say what she really thinks of Stanley.

Towards the end of the scene, Stanley is shown arriving outside, the noise of his approach covered conveniently by that of a train, and he is able to listen in to Blanche's diatribe against him, unseen both by Blanche and Stella. This gives Stanley the upper hand in his battle with Blanche. We see Stanley going back out and then pretending to have just arrived moments later.

After the relatively sedate Scene 4, which mostly comprises of a two-hander between Blanche and Stella, Scene 5 is full of movement and features a wider  range of characters and storylines. Most importantly, Williams has the young man Blanche flirts with and steals a kiss from exit just as Mitch enters the scene to take Blanche out on a date. If Mitch had entered the scene a little earlier, he would have been disabused of his impression that Blanche is a 'prim and proper' lady. Moreover, the replacement of the attractive young man with the Mitch on stage, highlights the latter's lack of youthful vibrancy. Although Blanche calls him her 'Rosenkavalier', we have already witnessed how awkward and clumsy Mitch can be in his attempts at gallantry and courtship.

After the business of Scene 5, which features many members of the cast and lots of comings and goings, Scene 6 is more quiet, settled and focused. The entire scene comprises a two-hander with only Blanche and Mitch on stage. The settled, uninterrupted quality, alongside other features such as the dim intimate lighting, conjure an atmosphere in which Blanche can reveal the central story in her tragedy, the death of her young husband, and the guilt she feels about this.

The dramatic irony in Scene 7 makes Blanche's entrance at the end of the scene more powerful. She has not heard Stanley revealing her disreputable life in Laurel to her sister and to us, the audience. The delay in Blanche's emergence from the bathroom to learn the bitter truth builds up the audience's anticipation. Then in one line of dialogue the actor playing Blanche has to go from giddy gaiety to desperate anxiety and something close to despair.

Mitch's failure to arrive for Blanche's birthday party, in Scene 8, undermines that celebration. His forceful entrance in Scene 9, where he pushes past Blanche into the bedroom, indicates his newly aggressive state of mind. When, at the end of the scene, Mitch tries to manhandle Blanche, she has to force his exit, by shouting 'Fire!' so that he 'clatters awkwardly down the steps' and is gone.

After the play's final exit, when Blanche is led-off by the Doctor and Matron, Stanley and Stella are left alone on stage. From the earlier dialogue, we know that Blanche has told Stella about the rape but, although she is clearly devastated by what is happening to her sister, it seems that Stella will not leave Stanley. Perhaps she didn't believe Blanche. Perhaps she dismissed what she said as another manifestation of her overactive imagination or a symptom of her incipient madness. Nevertheless, Williams' choice to have her stay with her brutal husband has proved controversial.

Interestingly, in the 1951 film version, the ending is changed. When Stanley reaches to touch Stella, she says, 'Don't you ever touch me again' and then, picking up the baby, starts to leave. After saying to herself that she is 'never going back, never' and as Stanley shouts after her, she runs upstairs to Eunice's flat.

Themes

Desire

It doesn't seem at all radical to suggest that the behaviour of human beings is driven as much by emotions as it is by reason. Nor, over a hundred years after Sigmund Freud was first articulating his theories of the mind, very radical to suggest that sometimes these emotions are not fully conscious ones, but semiconscious or even subconscious. Freud also argued that sexual desire, the libido, is a key driver, perhaps even *the* key driver, steering human behaviour. Probably that did seem a radical and controversial idea in the mid-twentieth century, particularly in terms of public discourse. Acknowledging such theories in academic circles was very different to depicting them in narrative form for consumption by the public, particularly on the stage and in cinemas. For more than half of the twentieth century, in the U.S.A and in England, presenting sexual desire in a novel or, even worse, on stage or screen, was often extremely problematic and could lead to censorship, as we already know from the treatment of Elia Kazan's 1951 film version of *Streetcar....*

Moreover, while the male libido may have been a problematic subject, the expression of female sexual desires was, for much of the twentieth century, almost entirely taboo.

Sometimes being frank about the nature and power of men and women's sexual desires could even be dangerous for writers, and their publishers. Nearly a decade after Williams wrote the play, the American poet and publisher Lawrence Ferlinghetti was arrested for publishing fellow poet, Allen Ginsberg's, long poem *Howl*, which the authorities had deemed obscene. Only after a protracted court case were the writers and the poem exonerated. In a similar case, a couple of years later, in England the publishers of D.H. Lawrence's novel *Lady Chatterley's Lover* were taken to court when the novel was labelled obscene under the Obscene Publications Act of 1959. The same novel had run into similar difficulties with the censors in the States.

Censorship of visual media, stage and film, was even tighter. Up until 1968 the Lord Chamberlain acted as censor to all plays performed on English stages. Over in the States, a sense of the level of censorship is illustrated by the interference with Edward Albee's play *Who's Afraid of Virginia Woolf*. When this play was turned into a film in 1966, the official censor insisted on the removal from the script of the word 'screw' as this was deemed obscene. This sort of intrusive and prudish censorship of films was abolished in the U.S.A. a few years later, also in 1968.

Hopefully such context helps us appreciate why Williams' play was considered shocking and radical when it was first written and performed. Because, as the title suggests, the behaviour of all the characters, and particularly the principal ones, both male and female, seems to be driven, primarily, by their libidos. Additionally, there is a sultry atmosphere throughout the play, evoked through the frequent references to heat, via the costumes, music and lighting and through the often charged interactions between characters, most especially between Blanche and Stanley. The claustrophobic feel of the flat, accentuated by the fact that all the scenes take place within its confines and the lack of solid partitions between spaces, intensifies the play's pervasive atmosphere of desire.

Despite her presentation of herself as demure and lady-like, Blanche cannot seem to control her sexual desires and they drive her to a series of transgressions. In particular, she is, of course, irresistibly attracted to young men. Even though she has lost her job as a teacher due to a relationship with a seventeen-year-old student, and despite the fact that she is waiting for Mitch to arrive to take her on a date, we see her acting in a seductive and predatory manner with the young man selling the Evening Star. Why she behaves in this way is never explained in the play, leaving a tempting gap for readers and audiences to fill with their theories. Some critics suggest that Blanche is intoxicated by the beauty of youth, by an innocence and purity she has lost. Though she cannot regain these qualities, through these relationships she can feel connected to youthful innocence. Perhaps this is linked to the trauma of losing her young husband – in some tragically warped way Blanche is trying to recover her connection to him through these transgressive relationships. Other critics read her behaviour more severely, arguing that Blanche preys on youthful men, like a vampire. In our section on the young man, later in this guide, we include Williams' own take on the matter.

Blanche herself provides one possible explanation for her promiscuity. Rather than desiring sexual pleasure for its own sake, she was, she tells Mitch, trying to find a cure for her desperate loneliness and to discover the protection she needed from the harsh realities of life: 'intimacies with strangers was all I seemed to fill my empty heart with... hunting for some protection... in the most – unlikely places'.

Of course, Blanche is not the most reliable of characters and despite these claims, there isn't one neat psychological explanation for her errant desires, and that surely is the point. She doesn't fully understand why she is driven to behave in this way  and neither do we. Mystery is at the heart of our desires. And as the title of the play suggests, like a streetcar, desires can carry us away to destinations unknown. What we do know is that desires are very hard to rationalise or contain and that they can lead characters such as Blanche and Stanley to do terrible things.

From their first encounter in the flat, it is clear that Blanche and Stanley are simultaneously repelled by and also attracted to each other. The long stage direction describing Stanley in Scene 1 concludes by saying that he 'sizes women up at a glance, with sexual classifications, crude images flashing his mind and determining the way he smiles at them'. Quickly then, he sizes Blanche up and from here on in, when he smiles at her, Stanley habitually 'grins' at Blanche. Used to male sexual attention, Blanche recognises straightaway the look he is giving her, 'drawing involuntarily back from his stare'. Moments later, Stanley makes an excuse to take off his shirt.

Understanding the nature of Stanley's grinning at her, Blanche could have sent clear signals to discourage him. Instead, she chooses to flirt provocatively. While in close proximity to Stanley, and with Stella outside the flat, she puts on and then takes off her red satin robe, asks Stanley to do her a 'favour', invites him to look at her, repeatedly encourages him to compliment her appearance, makes him do up the buttons on her dress and asks to share his cigarette, putting her lips where his lips have been. Then the conversation quickly turns to what Stanley finds attractive in women. When Blanche sprays herself with her 'atomizer', she 'playfully sprays him' too.

Though Blanche tries to cast her seductive spell on him, the stage directions indicate Stanley is very aware of what she is doing: his face has a 'smouldering look'; his voice is 'booming'; he 'seizes the atomizer and slams it down'. Is he angry or excited by Blanche's flirting? Both, at the same time, it seems. By nature, Stanley has trouble keeping his desires in check. They seem almost always about to break out into physical violence. This short scene sets up a dynamic that will, of course, conclude with the sexual violence he inflicts on Blanche in Scene 10.

Stanley's frustration at Blanche's continued presence in the flat is fed by many sources. One of the most potent is the frustration of his desire to set 'them coloured lights going' again. Clearly Blanche sleeping so close by has adversely affected his love life. Depending on how a production is staged, it may even be that she has moved in and occupied the couple's bedroom. Stanley's habitual roughness - the way he bangs and rips and hurls and slams everything he touches – can be read, in this way, as an expression of the frustration of his sexual desires.

Partly Blanche behaves in a sexually provocative manner with Stanley because she is trying to get the upper hand in a power play. She needs to win over Stanley and uses the method she knows best, seductive charm. But there is a sense too that, despite her protestations to the contrary, she is fatally attracted to him. Later, unaware that Stanley is listening to her, she rants about his bestiality - how he is like an 'animal', how he is 'ape-like', how he can only growl and grunt like a 'survivor of the Stone Age!'. So excessive is the description, it sounds like a form of self-persuasion. As she had admitted already to Stella, Blanche is powerfully attracted to Stanley's physical vigour: 'What such a man has to offer is animal force...' Shockingly, she concludes that '...the only way to live with such a man is to – go to bed with him!'

Williams doesn't present difficult-to-contain sexual desires as the preserve of men or of outsider characters, such as Blanche. Like her sister, Stella's behaviour seems to be controlled by desire. Though she recognises the many defects in her husband – his boorishness, his crudeness, his cruelty, his stupid violence – she also finds his behaviour exhilarating. Stella tells Blanche how on their wedding night Stanley 'smashed all the light-bulbs' with her slipper and that she found this violence thrilling. A little later, when Stella tells Blanche that there are certain 'things that happen between a man and a woman in the dark' and these 'make everything else seem unimportant', Blanche recognises she is talking about 'brutal desire – just – Desire!' Recognising something, particularly in others, is different, however, from recognising it, let alone addressing it, in ourselves.

It is the way in which Williams depicts desire, particularly sexual desire, as such a powerful driver of human behaviour that was, and still is, shocking. Blanche tells us that her 'grandfathers and uncles and brothers' lost Belle Reve due to their 'epic fornications'; Mitch is nearly driven to violence by his desire for Blanche; Allan Grey's life fell apart when he gave in to sexual desire; Blanche and Stella cannot control their sexual urges; Stanley's toxic desires drive him to commit rape. Boldly, for a play of its time, *Streetcar...* shows desire to be a force just as irresistible for the female characters as it is for the men. Presented as an ungovernable, transgressive, violent force, it is so potent that it cannot be contained or restrained by reason or morality, by social mores or civilised values. Whether it is through Stanley's whirling 'coloured lights' or Blanche's sensual description of her desire for the young man - 'you make my mouth water' - Williams makes the primitive hold desires have on both men and women vividly and troublingly tangible.

Eros and Thanatos

According to Sigmund Freud, in his essay *Beyond the Pleasure Principle* published in 1920, all instincts fall into one of two major classes: life drives and death drives—later dubbed Eros and Thanatos by other psychologists.

Eros is considered to be the drive to live which encapsulates the desire to be part of a social framework, to reproduce and to survive. Thanatos on the other hand is the inexorable drive towards death which encompasses risky behaviour, reliving past trauma and aggression. The two drives have a tricky relationship but in *Streetcar...* they offer an interesting way to consider the qualities of Stella and Blanche.

If we think about what 'drives' Stella, it is clear that escaping Belle Reve the 'summer dad died' is key to understanding her motivation. The old plantation is imbued with death and the lively, modernity of New Orleans offers a more life affirming alternative. Early in the play Stella asserts that 'The best I could do was to make my own living,' which emphasises her determination to break free from the shackles of the deep south and enter into a world where she can work for her own money. Clearly, she is a survivor. When the play opens, we see her new home in a shared house within a down-at-heel, working-class neighbourhood. It is a long way from the gentility of a southern plantation. Naturally Blanche is disgusted at what she considers to be squalid 'living conditions', but Stella, unlike Blanche, has, at least, a roof over her head.

In terms of fitting into a social network, Stella has been assimilated successfully into the world inhabited by Stanley. She hasn't tried to change to fit in - clearly her neighbours know about her aristocratic past - but she is largely comfortable in her own skin. As we've discussed in other parts of this guide, there are moments when she speaks in the language of her upbringing but, equally, she is content to read popular comic books after her night of passion with Stanley, rather than the improving literature Blanche commends. She and Stanley interact with their neighbours and when Steve and Eunice have a huge argument, Stella comments, when Eunice goes to get a drink from the Four Deuces, that that is 'much more practical' than going to the police about the altercation. We also hear about her sending over a custard to Mitch's sick mother and there are countless other examples of Stella's pragmatism, such as taking Blanche out for the evening during the poker party. She understands that the women need to keep out of the way and she accommodates Stanley's friends even if she finds their poker-playing tiresome. Stella's philosophy is one of stoicism and tolerance. She has adjusted herself in the name of survival.

Stella's sexual relationship with Stanley is also crucial in terms of understanding her drives. First of all, she is married to Stanley - this is no one-night stand - so again this reinforces Stella's willingness to fit social norms. Despite other 'issues' in their relationship, Stella is clearly 'crazy' about Stanley, recounting how she 'nearly go[es] wild' when he is away. Their physical relationship is made very clear in Scene 4 when Stella appears drugged by her night of passion with Stanley. Additionally, Stella is pregnant which also conforms to 'Eros' in which the desire to procreate is seen as a drive to perpetuate the life force.

And Stanley himself, with his physical vigour and his rough sort of joie de vivre and his role of 'gaudy seed-bearer', embodies the life force of 'Eros'. When things come to their inevitable crisis, Stella chooses him and their baby at the expense of her sister.

Blanche, on the other hand, can be seen as the embodiment of 'Thanatos' - the death instinct. Although she arrives on a streetcar named 'Desire' she has transferred to 'one called Cemeteries'. And, although she has left death-ridden 'Belle Reve' behind, it still haunts her imagination. The symbolism of The Varsouviana, which plays at moments in which memory overwhelms her, signals Blanche's inability to escape from past traumas. The fact that it is punctuated by 'a shot' shows how indelibly Allan's suicide is imprinted on her mind and it is evident that this formative experience has shaped Blanche's behaviour ever since. The Mexican woman selling 'Flores para los muertos' is another reminder of Blanche's close connection with death and it is significant that when Blanche tries to 'confess' to Stella, Stella doesn't listen, telling Blanche that she is being 'morbid'.

Towards the end of the play, when Blanche's promiscuity has been exposed, she tries to explain how she needed 'intimacies with strangers' to fill her 'empty heart with' and how 'panic drove' her 'from one to another hunting for some protection'. This confession contrasts to Stella's fruitful liaison with Stanley; Blanche's encounters are unfulfilling, fleeting and lead nowhere but down. This sexual behaviour becomes increasingly risky which is synonymous with the Thanatos drive. Blanche's use of alcohol is similarly risky. A misdirected kind of self-medication to numb pain, it only lowers her inhibitions and fuels memories of times past, as can be seen when she propositions the young man collecting for the Evening Star. And this predatory behaviour too can be read through the perspective of Thanatos, with Blanche acting like a gothic vampire attracted to the vitality of youth.

Indeed, aggression is another part of the Thanatos drive. While it might seem strange to discuss Blanche in terms of aggression, there are plenty of examples, culminating in the breaking of the bottle in Scene 10. At this point Blanche is only threatened by Stanley's proximity; he hasn't touched her and nor has he threatened to. Arguably, it is the breaking of the bottle and Blanche's declaration that she will 'twist the broken end' in his face that provokes Stanley into violence.

The snare of the past prevents Blanche from moving forward. The trauma of her marriage and the gothic horror of the demise of the inhabitants of Belle Reve keep her in thrall. The description of the last days of Belle Reve are of a 'long parade to the graveyard' where 'death was as close as you are'. Blanche fixates on the 'blood-stained pillow slips' and the deaths of 'Father, Mother, Margaret, that dreadful way! So big with it, it couldn't be put in a coffin! But had to be burned like rubbish!' By contrast, she imagines her own death as clinical, but also cyclical: 'When I die, I'm going to die on the sea... And I'll be buried at sea sewn up in a clean white sack and dropped overboard - at noon - in the blaze of summer and into an ocean as blue as my first lover's eyes.' Although she is attracted by youth, by vitality and by life, ultimately Blanche is not strong enough to break free from the traumas of her past and the bony grip the southern gothic.

Illusion and reality

Question: What's the difference between an illusion and a delusion? Sounds like some intellectual joke but it's not. It's part of an important process or exchange in the play. An illusion is a misleading representation of reality, 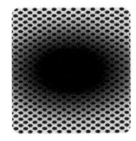 created in an effort to hide that reality, whereas a delusion is to be tricked, the desired effect of the illusion. Illusion is the cause; delusion is the effect. So, in *Streetcar...* what are the illusions, who creates these illusions, why do they create illusions, who are they trying to delude: other people, themselves? What's so wrong with reality that illusions are so prevalent in the play? Why does Williams construct such a large imaginative space to explore illusions and delusions in his play? Even before the play begins, Williams' epigraph quoting the modernist poet Hart Crane points to the strong presence of illusions in life. From Crane's poem *The Broken Tower*, the quatrain quoted alludes to a fall from paradise and the loss of innocence, the transitory nature of love and the isolation of humans in the chaos of life.

> And so it was I entered the broken world
> To trace the visionary company of love, its voice
> An instant in the wind [I know not whither hurled]
> But not for long to hold each desperate choice.

Here Williams forewarns the audience/reader about the illusion of innocence needing to be smashed by reality. Love itself is something that needs to be followed or chased, and by using the adjective 'visionary' Crane foregrounds love as something fanciful or impractical. In other words, love appears to be an elusive illusion that may be chased but is never caught. The illusion of love appears to be a narcotic that makes reality endurable and offers only a fleeting but addictive consolation. Shortly the addict will be desperately craving another hit. Illusions then, from the very onset of the play, exert great power, narratively and thematically.

Clearly, Blanche is the chief creator of illusions, deceiving firstly others, then herself. Or is it first herself, then others, then herself so completely that she is no longer able to discern illusion from reality? That sounds about right. What exactly is Blanche deluding the other characters about? With Blanche there is evasion and there is illusion. The first of these is the withholding of the truth, whereas the other is outright lying and deception. In the main, Blanche resorts to evasiveness because she has a difficult personal history to hide and once this tactic fails she resorts to illusions. Her promiscuity and reckless immorality have basically destroyed her social reputation, her connection to her home and ultimately her sense of self. So, she evades and lies to prevent others discovering a reality that shames her. When the revelation about Belle Reve being 'lost' occurs in Scene 1, Blanche deflects close inspection of her version of events by accusing Stella of selfishly absconding. Her affronted martyr performance is quite effective; Stella accepts her version of events with very little fuss: 'Oh it had to be - sacrificed or something'. Blanche's evasions, however, cannot withstand the relentless questioning and probing of Stanley, a man who demands truth presented plain and simple, a laying of 'cards on the table': 'Now let's skip back a little to where you said the place in the country was disposed of'. Unfortunately, for Blanche, evasion is simply not enough to survive in a Stanley-dominated environment, and this leads to her resorting to illusions.

It is unsurprising really that Blanche is so fond of illusion as she is a scion of genteel Southern plantation owners. Belle Reve is nothing but an illusion in itself, a symbol of civilisation hiding a reality of exploitative slavery, inhumane racism and capitalist greed behind a whitewashed veneer of sophistication, culture and progress. But, as the play also reveals, it is a remarkably tenacious illusion, with a cultural feeling of loss remaining in the collective white Southern imagination almost a century after the American Civil War.

On a personal level, as opposed to a cultural level, Blanche's fondness for illusion is symbolised from the very start by her wardrobe trunk, a target of Stanley's ire in Scene 2. This trunk is full of the legal debris of Belle Reve's dissolution, the yellowed love poetry of her doomed husband, Allan Gray, but more importantly the costume of the Southern Belle, the refined and sophisticated leisure lady Blanche dreams of being. Stanley's disgust at these items - 'feathers and furs', a 'solid gold dress', 'genuine fox-fur pieces, a half a mile long' and so forth - is reflected in his disgusted manhandling of them, each one symbolising money syphoned out of his pocket. Ironically, Stanley is deluded here, which is as Blanche would want. But it is only due to his ignorance, and it is temporary. He thinks that her extravagant, sartorial opulence, is the explanation for the loss of 'your plantation, or what's left of it!'. However, Stella knows what Stanley cannot: that these are just fragments of a costume Blanche has assembled to play her character. What Stanley thinks in 'the treasure chest of a pirate' is only fake *costume jewellery*. In a rough-and-tumble place like the French Quarter, it's convincing enough for Blanche to make a new start. Illusion for her is a shield, a protection against the intrusion of harsh realities.

But not only does Blanche possess the costume she needs, she also possesses the consummate acting skills of an expert illusionist. Her positioning of Mitch as a viable romantic saviour, her 'Rosenkavalier', revolves around a compelling illusion: Blanche as the demure, refined and highly respectable beauty ['He hasn't gotten a thing but a goodnight kiss, that's all I have given him. I want his respect'.] She plays the role so well, using her love of poetry and her more refined upbringing to dazzle Mitch into believing that romance between them is possible. But only if it is a pure, fairy-tale romance, because of her 'old-fashioned ideals'. The illusion is so enchanting that even Blanche starts to believe that Mitch may be the man capable of supplying the 'kindness' that she so desperately seeks. Even in the midst of her role- playing, she is, however, arch and partially self-aware: When she espouses her old-fashioned ideals '*she rolls her eyes*', slipping momentarily out of character. The dramatic irony here is amusing to the audience but it also reveals her as a practical opportunist, deluding poor dopey Mitch for her own benefit. Here, illusion is purely selfish and duplicitous, a pretence aimed at profit.

Williams also expertly manipulates the audience into thinking that this romance has potential. Despite Blanche's many faults and her deceptions, the audience desires happiness for her. Mitch also is cleverly positioned as 'superior' to his buddies, allowing the possibility of a mutually beneficial match. But, ultimately, Williams deludes us for the purpose of drama. The explosive rejection of Blanche as wife in Scene 9 sees her illusions shattered. No longer a potential wife, she is reduced to the sex object she was in Laurel, a mere consumable with Mitch 'fumbling to embrace her'. This rejection brings crisis into Blanche's life as her preference for 'magic' over 'realism' is revealed to be both delusional and immoral. So, who exactly is she deluding here? It's a complex situation. While the 'same old act, same old lines, same old hooey' point to a tired performance, it's clear that her deception is driven by a deep desperation to rewrite the past. In a patriarchal world in which 'men don't – don't even admit your existence unless they are making love to you', she wants to escape her disreputable past by playing the role of 'a lily'. She creates a precarious, alternative reality where 'magic' reigns, where 'what ought to be the truth' rather than truth is presented. It's deception, but it's well-intentioned deception. Blanche gives Mitch what she thinks he wants but also, crucially, what she wants for herself: desirability and respect.

A different play might have let her away with this. But Streetcar... is a tragedy. Williams' end for Blanche is much more annihilating than simply the  symbolic tearing down of the Chinese paper lantern and the harsh glare of reality that reveals Blanche to be a 'fading' beauty. Both Mitch and Stanley 'tear down' the symbolic paper lantern, to point a remorseless, judgemental beam at Blanche's life. Defensively, she has had to 'turn the trick' and 'put on soft colours, the colours of butterfly wings, and glow - make a little - temporary magic' simply just to survive the 'storm' of reality. In other words, illusion is a means of survival for a vulnerable woman in a harsh male-dominated world. The 'kindness' Blanche so desperately seeks is nowhere to be found in the play and these truth-loving men crush her and the magic and kindness she values so highly. Blanche may use illusion to survive but she is ultimately harmless. The punishment for her 'crime' of trying to weave a dream out of fragments of memories and fantasies is serious sexual assault and mental unravelling. To state the facts Stanley-style, Blanche lies and Stanley rapes, yet she is incarcerated, while he escapes justice. Whereas previously Blanche constructed illusions to hide in, eventually illusion and reality become dangerously and impossibly intertwined.

The traumatic sequence of the intensifying 'Varsouviana polka' and 'the distant revolver shot' that soundtracks Blanche's memories of Allan Gray's suicide in Scene 1 and Scene 6, begins to change in Scene 8. This moment signifies when Blanche's exhausted mind can no longer bear reality. Stanley's brutal birthday present of a bus ticket back to Laurel banishes Blanche back to a world where her illusions are transparent, like the emperor's new clothes. Appropriately, given that he's never been deluded by Blanche's various performances for a second, Stanley's cruel puncturing of her illusions is fitting but vicious and she begins to fracture mentally in the face of his unkindness. So traumatic is Stanley's message that she's to be flung back to Laurel that at the end of Scene 8, she starts speaking in tongues, almost [well, Spanish anyway!]. It's unclear why she is speaking in Spanish and who exactly she is impersonating, but her whispered repetition of 'the cornbread, the cornbread, the unsalted cornbread' while 'twisting a washcloth' make her akin to a domestic servant of the type that she may encountered in her affluent youth. This is the first time that her illusions seem to be out of her control, or certainly that they make no sense, given what she wants to achieve. The ambiguity of these words could relate to having to face an 'unsalted' reality, i.e. a reality devoid of illusions, or it could refer to her own 'fading' status as a woman plain and unadorned. Either way, Blanche's airy illusions have now become darker, almost hallucinations.

Her mental deterioration continues in Scene 9 where her 'Rosenkavalier is replaced by an unshaven, drunken Mitch with 'a face like a thundercloud'. For the first time in the play, it becomes explicit that Blanche's imagination is the source of the Varsouviana. She thanks Mitch for stopping that 'polka tune that I had caught in my head'. Later on, Mitch is forced to ask 'what music?'. His asking whether she is 'boxed out of her mind' is Williams' unsubtle signal for the audience: she's struggling here! The illusion of Mitch as her saviour dies quickly and with it the destruction of any chances for 'rest [and] to breathe quietly again'. However, while Blanche's mind fractures here, it doesn't completely shatter until Scene 10.

The rape is the nightmare catalyst that causes illusion to tip into full-blown delusions and terrifying hallucinations: her dream of holidaying with Shep Huntleigh, a fantasy upgrade of Mitch, becomes a safer, alternative reality she cannot or will not exit. She becomes trapped inside her own illusions, deluding herself [willingly or unwillingly isn't exactly clear] to escape harsh reality. Her hallucinations become multi-sensory. It's not just the sounds of trauma that haunt her, and the sounds intensify to include 'inhuman voices like cries in a jungle', it's also the visuals of trauma. Williams' uses Expressionistic flourishes to externalise her internal mental landscape: 'lurid reflections appear on the walls; the shadows are of a grotesque and menacing form [and] move sinuously as flames along the wall spaces.' Not all productions use these Expressionistic directions. Elia Kazan's 1947 version, for instance, jettisoned them in preference for a gritty realism. Even if they are rejected, Blanche's appearance at the start of Scene 10 suggests a steep mental unravelling: she appears a grotesque parody, a degraded fantasy of her own illusion, as she pathetically sits alone, drunk, 'in a somewhat soiled and crumpled white satin evening gown and a pair of scuffed silver slippers'.

The theatre critic Wolcott Gibbs, in a 1947 review of the original Elia Kazan production, identified here 'a mind desperately retreating into the beautiful, crazy world it has built for itself'. Thus, illusion becomes self-delusion, and the dark message of the play is that sometimes reality is so traumatising that self-delusion is the only escape. The only problem for Blanche is that this escape seems involuntary and irreversible; her escape becomes an imprisonment.

Williams clearly provokes the audience into contemplating the nature of justice in the playworld and to consider whether Blanche's 'crimes' deserve the punishment doled out to her. If this is justice at work then clearly justice itself is an illusion, constructed by the uncaring 'hard ones' that Blanche knows must be appeased. Coupled with the doomed battle she fights against uncontrollable, stronger forces, the disproportionate nature of her punishment transforms her into a tragic heroine. Like a tragic hero, she is culpable too: her own actions stained her reputation in Laurel, but Williams makes it undeniable *why* she did this. As a tragic hero, she also has a hamartia

– an inability to face reality and a reliance on illusions. Williams makes her motivations clear and comprehensible so that it's very difficult not to sympathise with her at the end as she is led like a child from the apartment. Williams' treatment of Blanche suggests that illusions must be used to combat unpalatable realities, to provide refuges, but that an overreliance on them can destabilise a person's ability to distinguish reality from illusion. He also suggests that it is the 'soft ones' like Blanche that need illusions much more than the 'hard ones' like Stanley. These opposing forces of illusion and reality are symbolised by the clash between Blanche and Stanley. Ultimately, Stanley wins and in doing so foists the need for illusion on another woman: his wife. Stella is forced to delude herself with the illusion that her sister's accusations of rape are insanity and that her husband is an honourable man. Elia Kazan quite rightly pondered the logic of Williams' play in his director's notes: 'Are we going into the era of Stanley? He may be practical and right*…but what…does it leave us?'

It leaves us in a new America, founded on, and promoting, brutality, viciousness, unkindness, cruelty. The reality of this new America, the play seems to say, is founded on misguided illusions of civilisation. And the American Dream is revealed to be a nightmare. Indeed, America itself, it seems, is a delusion.

[* highly debatable]

America

Regarded by many critics as Williams' most successful play and itself an iconic part of American culture, *A Streetcar Named Desire* not only presents us with a staggeringly rich picture of life in 1940s New Orleans, but also has some compelling things to say about that ubiquitous thematic concern: the American Dream. Unlike his predecessors, literary heavyweights like John Steinbeck and F. Scott  Fitzgerald, Williams depicts a fast-changing, post-World War 2 America in which 'the dream' is arguably coming true for some, albeit at the expense of others.

What then does *Streetcar...* have to say about the place in which it is set? As we have said, everything that happens is rooted in the reality of New Orleans, with actual place names, such as Elysian Fields and Cemeteries, as well as the titular tram which really did run 'between the L&N tracks and the river'. There is an abundance of reality in this play. There are American Jax beers and bowling alleys, jazz and blues, cokes, poker games and five-dollar bills. It's hardly surprising that the picture we get is so realistic, given that Tennessee Williams had been born and raised in Mississippi, and moved to New Orleans when he was 28. His intimate knowledge of the setting he describes in such detail in the stage directions, and the concrete sense of a gritty, unmanicured, 'warts and all' lifestyle, create an effective contrast with the effete fantasy world that Blanche brings with her from Belle Reve.

When Blanche arrives from her hometown of Laurel, she is not prepared for the 'New America' she finds. The 'conditions' in which Stella is living do not live up to her sister's rather snobbish expectations, coming as she does from a much less tolerant, less ethnically diverse part of the country. Most critics agree that Blanche represents the Old South, adhering in vain to a set of values that had begun dying out after the American Civil war of 1861-1865. We know from the clothes Blanche wears and the way she speaks that she is different. Although it is mostly affected, her behaviour and way of speaking reflect a much more refined and privileged upbringing than that of characters like Eunice or Stanley. Blanche likes to imagine herself as the 'Southern Belle', like Scarlett O'Hara in the film *Gone with the Wind*. But, having lost the family home, a loss she puts down to the 'epic fornications' of her predecessors, Blanche can afford none of the trappings that go with such an image. Her jewellery is fake, her costumes tacky. By the time she arrives in Elysian Fields, Belle Reve is no more than its name suggests, a beautiful dream. Blanche's dream is stuck in the past.

The modern, urban America, or rather this specific French Quarter of New Orleans, which provides the play's backdrop, represents a country which has changed radically. Since the Civil War, colonial values had gradually been replaced by those adopted by a new industrialised, more robust and diverse society. In the title and throughout the play, Williams often invokes the sound of the streetcar, and also the locomotive train. As well as being symbols of desire, both are powerful signs of the industrial progress that had been made in the early nineteenth century. After WW2, this process rapidly accelerated. Immigration rates rose sharply. Stanley Kowalski, Blanche's brother-in-law, to whom she refers derogatorily as a 'Polak', is the vigorous embodiment of the success, not the failure, of the American Dream. The son of a Polish immigrant, he has fought in the war for his country and feels staunchly patriotic and determined to make it. He likes a gamble and he's a winner. All the qualities we come to associate with Stanley - no-nonsense, straight-talking, brute-force - we might easily connect with the kind of tough post-war American culture Williams depicts in this play.

In terms of genre, in many ways *Streetcar...* defies categorisation, however most critics would probably consider it 'Southern Gothic'. This is because it is an evolution of what other American writers like Edgar Allan Poe, to whom Blanche actually refers in scene 1, had begun in the previous century. Horrified by the kind of neighbourhood in which Stella now lives, Blanche exclaims: 'Never, never, never in my worst dreams could I picture - Only Poe...could do it justice!' By this, she suggests that Elysian Fields, far from being a paradise, is dark and frightening - the backdrop for horrifying events. Indeed, she even calls it a 'horrible place'. Southern Gothic typically explores the decline of the American 'nobility' and often presents the reader with macabre and disturbing events, charting characters' psychological, as well as their physical, demise. This is certainly what we see in Blanche's story. It is not difficult to make the leap from Blanche's downfall to that of her anachronistic, Old American, way of life.

At the end of the play, the new order wins the battle played out metaphorically between Blanche and Stanley. And it is a violent defeat. As Blanche is raped by Stanley, so the New America symbolically asserts its power over the old Southern way of life. Through the drama, Williams presents the audience with a choice: hang on to the old or embrace the new. Stella chooses the latter and, in so doing, sacrifices her only surviving relation. She opts for a world of Mexican tamale sellers, Spanish and Polish immigrants, white and black people all living together in what Williams calls an 'easy intermingling of races'. In many ways, it seems like a good choice. It is an unpretentious, tolerant world, a far cry from the life of segregation experienced by many immigrants in other parts of America at that time and, indeed, for two decades or more afterwards. As with so many things in this play, however, nothing is straightforward. This New America is far from perfect - it is a 'dog-eat-dog' world in which you have to be brutal and ruthless to survive. In the play's closing line, just after Blanche is removed to an asylum, Steve starts the next game of poker: 'This game is seven card stud'. His indifference to Blanche's fate is shocking, but it sends out a clear message that, in this New America, 'life goes on'.

Critical Commentaries

Scenes 1-3

Welcome to New Orleans, French Quarter, aka Elysian Fields, a place where money is tight, space is cramped, the music is constant, the noise is palpable and 'where there is a relatively warm and easy intermingling of the races'. The heavy lifting done by the word 'relatively' here is significant, given the context of the virulently racist American South in 1947. This is a play where violence and crime simmer just around every corner. Ultimately, the playworld is a space where passions and desires throb,
 endlessly aching for satisfaction. The temperature is set to SWEAT, with the relentless heat signifying sexual heat, hot-headed violence and guilt-ridden anxiety. Despite these seeming negativities, the place exudes a *'raffish charm,'* balancing on the border between bohemian and impoverished, thriving and overpopulated.

The playwright's imagination soars in his long lyrical stage directions, directions that expand leisurely into both the symbolic and the sensual. Like any literary text with a vibrant sense of place, the setting in the play is often seen as a character of sorts, but really it's more like a pressure chamber here, amplifying and accelerating character action and narrative intensity. Williams' stage directions are highly sensual: the sky is a *'tender blue, almost turquoise'*; *the warm breath of the brown river* can almost be felt; the river warehouses fill the air with suggestions of *'bananas and coffee'*; the air is full of the *'tinny ... 'Blue Piano' played with the infatuated fluency of brown fingers'* As we said in our section on stagecraft and will say again, good luck to any set designer seriously trying to capture the heady atmosphere Williams had in mind.

Before the central character Blanche DuBois arrives, Williams provides a swift vignette that serves to introduce the easy familiarity of the residents of Elysian Fields and the thrumming desires that are openly expressed here. The sailors looking for a 'clip joint' and the shouting vendor selling 'Red hots!' articulate the pleasure-seeking that seems so central in the play. There also is a nifty snapshot of the intensity of Stella and Stanley's marriage with him *'bellowing'* and her *'mildly'* remonstrating with him. Williams certainly makes us very aware of Stanley as a hunter-gatherer-protector type, with his heaving of a 'red-stained package from a butcher's' to his wife.

Into this coarse yet energetic world steps Blanche, an incongruous blow-in from another world. As we've mentioned elsewhere in this guide, one of Williams' working titles for this play was *The Moth* and his stage directions demand that visually and physically she *'suggests a moth'*. As the play starts, her all-white exterior points to her out-of-place cleanliness in a dirty, busy, urban setting but also to a visual purity, which retrospectively, is highly ironic. The moth-like qualities of this woman also suggest frailty [she has a *'delicate beauty'*], a certain jitteriness of movement and also makes her a night-creature, a lover of the dusky light and dark shadows. What is more interesting in this opening is the information about the characters' ages. Traditionally in theatrical productions, Blanche is usually imagined to be in her forties, but some basic maths here reveals that Stella is 25, Stanley 28 to 30 and Blanche is 30 [by the end of the play 31], which is a long way from the over-the-hill beauty that haunts her imagination. This certainly makes the repressed sexual attraction that is supposed to exist between Blanche and Stanley more understandable but makes her vanity nigh-on hysterical, which must be the point. Blanche is not remotely old, but her neurosis about ageing, and the destruction of the external validation she so desperately craves, makes her old.

This preoccupation with the death of her desirability is neatly symbolised in her directions to Stella's house directions. Brought to New Orleans by the phallic streetcar 'Desire', Blanche has had to pass death ['Cemeteries'] and has landed in the afterlife of 'Elysian Fields'. It's all so memorably symbolic! Blanche's character arc through the play criticises her enslavement to sexual desire, which will kill her reputation and appears to be symptomatic of a wider moral deterioration of the old plantation-owning classes from which she comes. As we've already noted in this guide, the Elysian Fields in classical mythology was a space for dead heroes. Blanche certainly doesn't fit this and by the play's end she is unceremoniously booted out of Elysian Fields for good.

Obviously, in Scene 1 we're here for the intros. Who are our main characters, what type of personalities do they have and how do they get on with each other? First-off, Blanche comes across as an entitled snob, as encapsulated by her brusque responses to the lowly characters of Eunice Hubbel and the Negro Woman. It's as if Blanche feels herself so distant from these unrefined city types that she cannot bear to even exchange civilities with them. Her rudeness becomes so obvious that she has to explain that 'I'd like to be left alone' to Eunice, who, understandably, is offended. It's an important insight into Blanche's superior attitude, something that becomes increasingly vocal as the play progresses, with dire results. However, to create some sympathy for her, Williams also shows Blanche as on the edge, in a state of high stress, which is brilliantly captured in her body language, with 'her shoulders slightly hunched', 'her leg pressed close together' while her hands are 'tightly clutching her purse'. With her exclamation that 'I've got to keep hold of myself' she makes explicit what the body language implies. The source of this stress is left 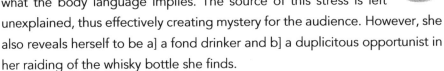 unexplained, thus effectively creating mystery for the audience. However, she also reveals herself to be a] a fond drinker and b] a duplicitous opportunist in her raiding of the whisky bottle she finds.

However, these deft brush strokes of characterisation are broadened as Williams has Blanche explode into performance of a familiar persona: the joyous, jittery Southern Belle, entertaining in her 'feverish vivacity'. Stella's arrival on stage is almost a trigger for this highly kinetic performance. Blanche's speeches come in an 'uneasy rush' and are much longer compared to the calmer, more measured Stella [rarely more than a single line, and often merely several words]. Sometimes Blanche's exaggerated responses are played for laughs, and there is a lot of potential comedy to be mined in this scene, but at times Blanche's persona totters into plain irritating - this was especially true of Gillian Anderson's performance in Benedict Andrews' 2014 production, which rendered Blanche as irritating as Stanley must have seen her. Note especially the melodramatic gestures of the panto actor: *'she touches her forehead shakily'*. Blanche's conversation is bordering on the frantic in its stops and starts and sudden lurches in topic: from Stella's rundown life ['that you had to live in these conditions'] to her own enviable figure ['I haven't put on one ounce in ten years!'] to her stinging reproach that Stella abandoned her to look after their crumbling ancestral home, Belle Reve ['all the burden descended on my shoulders!']).

The most compelling speech in this entire scene is Blanche's account of her tribulations at Belle Reve. It is as hyperbolic and fanciful as you'd expect from this highly-strung, self-centred woman. The language of this speech also reveals her training as an English teacher and an expert in emotive narratives. The intensely emotional nature of her speech is obvious in its flow of exclamations [24 exclamation marks in total!], progressing structurally from recounting her own acute distresses to accusing Stella of abandoning family duty for indulgent sexual satisfaction. Of course, this entire speech reduces 'the loss' of Belle Reve, their ancestral home, to minor exposition in the wildfire of Blanche's martyrdom. It is breathless in its febrile rhythms: it is full of other voices, forlorn and pathetic ['Don't let me go!']; accusing questions stabbing in their brevity; antithetical images of noisy death and quiet goodbyes; bitter humour about the Grim reaper putting 'his tent on our doorstep!'; the dramatic use of hyphens suggesting other things about to be said but then not. It's stirring stuff and certainly achieves its intended effect: to silence any questions about *how* Belle Reve was lost.

However, unfortunately for Blanche, a character who won't allow anyone to 'pull any wool over this boy's eyes' arrives and both Blanche and the audience get a much longer look at him than at the start of this scene. The first thing notable about Williams' stage directions, and it would have been apparent from his brief cameo earlier, is Stanley's *'animal'* magnetism. He doesn't just simply move, the verbs Williams uses to describe his movements are invariably dynamic and violent: he '<u>throws</u> the screen door open,' he '<u>heaves</u> the package at her' etc and this continues to the very end of the play. Williams presents the ultimate man's man, a potent concentration of machismo and sexual vigour. He is crude, but shrewd, an objectifier of women, reducing them to 'sexual classifications' and 'crude images'. Not only this, but he is loud, garish, vulgar and proud of it. Williams describes him as animated by the 'power and pride of a richly feathered male bird among hens'. Everything he does promotes the 'image of the gaudy seed bearer'. A pleasure-seeking and pleasure-loving man, in odd ways Stanley connects deeply with Blanche but ultimately he embodies an opposite to her fantastical notions of sophistication.

There are several notable things here in this first interchange that characterise him throughout the rest of the play. Firstly, is the way he stares and grins at Blanche: it is intimidating and disconcerting. Secondly, he repeatedly asks short, probing questions. Here, he asks 12 questions in this short interchange, revealing a relentless hunger for the truth, or to use his own lingo: a desire to cut the crap! The tension between Blanche and Stanley is captured in their very short lines, which closely resemble the rapid stichomythia of classical tragedy. It's a far shout from Blanche's previous chitter-chatter with her sister. In some ways it resembles a tense sizing-up between two adversaries, or maybe even a predator and prey where these roles have not been quite crystallised yet. Additionally, tension is created by the fact that Stanley is caught completely unawares: he doesn't know Blanche is coming to stay with them and he certainly doesn't know how long she will be staying. As the constant questions suggest, he is not a man who likes to be without convincing answers. And he certainly won't wait long for those answers: they'll be given or he's going to find out for himself.

In this scene, ultimately, Stanley shows his sharp powers of observation in noting how fast his liquor is disappearing and his powers of disruption as an agent of chaos. His constant questions bring Blanche to a disorientating collision with the traumatic past. The traumatic failure of her teenage marriage with 'the boy' is pulled brutally back into the present, making her declare that 'I'm afraid I'm - going to be sick!'. This traumatic memory is always soundtracked by the music of the polka, a highly effective Expressionistic flourish from Williams. It is a dramatic way to end this scene and begins a strategy that ensures we know this is Blanche's play and no one else's: we hear what she hears, but other characters do not hear and she nearly always ends each scene with some sort of dramatic statement or memorable act. The only other character who has the power to disrupt this narrative strategy is Stanley, which he does in Scenes Four, Ten and Eleven. This cements his status as the antagonist in the play.

A great thing about this play is its sense of claustrophobia. For a woman who wants to get away from the chaos of her own life and needs time and space to work out what to do next, Blanche couldn't have ended up in a worse place. Williams ensures this through the a) the relentless bustle of his New Orleans setting but also b) the cramped apartment, which houses two estranged sisters, one unborn baby and one prowling, domineering man. Whether outdoors or indoors, Blanche is assaulted from all sides by forces beyond her own control. Keeping the play within this pressure cooker turns up the tension and leads to explosive moments of drama.

The function of **Scene 2** is to deepen the antagonism between Blanche and Stanley and entrench Stella in the role of exasperated peacekeeper. Blanche is taking one of her many long baths as the scene opens. This serves a dual purpose: firstly, it serves to enrich Blanche's characterisation as a rather inconsiderate, high-maintenance leisure lady and, secondly, it serves a practical dramatic function in keeping her off stage while delivering some delicious dramatic irony for the audience. A long conversation between Stella and Stanley takes up roughly half of this scene and it also clarifies their relationship and characterisation. Stella is breezy and nimble in her efforts not to annoy her husband, while Stanley displays the same ruthless pursuit of answers displayed in Scene 1. Again, note the constant questions [over 40 in this scene alone!] Stanley peppers the conversation with. They are shorn of any descriptive language, functional in the extreme. Add in the inarticulate 'huh' that enters his questioning, and we get the picture of a man barely bothered with speech and certainly not bothered about engaging with pretty pleasantries.

What's he asking so many questions about? Revealingly, it's about money or in this case 'the Napoleonic code according to which what belongs to the wife belongs to the husband and vice versa'. The loss of Belle Reve represents a substantial loss of revenue to this working-class man, and he can't afford to be as flippant about it as Blanche and Stella are. The difference in their origins become clear: the women are used to having money and it being a renewable resource; he is not used to money and must scrabble to seize it and keep it. Stanley's ability to go from his default setting of mildly simmering to erupting volcano in nanoseconds is displayed here for the first time: Stella's vagueness about the loss of Belle Reve, Blanche's trunkful of extravagant 'fox-fur pieces half a mile long' and the lack of 'papers' infuriate him. His crude, biting sense of humour also appears for the first time, revealing a character who can be amusing but only on his terms, like Tommy DeVito in Scorsese's *Goodfellas*: laugh with, not at! His deliberate hyperbole fuels this bitter

 humour towards his sister-in-law: 'there's thousands of dollars invested in this stuff!'; 'the treasure chest of a pirate!'; 'What is this sister of yours? A deep-sea diver who brings up sunken treasures?' His violent invasion of Blanche's privacy is shockingly disrespectful: he '<u>jerks</u> out an armful of dresses', '<u>hurls</u> the furs to the daybed, '<u>pulls</u> up a fist-full of costume jewellery,' '<u>kicks</u> the trunk partly closed'. It would be difficult for an audience to side with this display of ignorance, an ignorance gently mocked by the play in his getting worked up about costume jewellery and not knowing what rhinestones are.

His cruelty too is clear for all to see. Not just content to stay silent when Blanche arrives, instantly he goes on the offensive. He will not cooperate with Stella's pleas for basic manners, certainly not when she orders him to. The second half of the scene is Stanley harassing Blanche until he finds what he wants, which, ironically, he doesn't find anyway. It's all a waste of time but it is a memorable display of his relentlessness and brutal indifference. His swift deflation of Blanche's hopes for a flattering compliment is characteristic: 'I don't go in for that stuff'. Stanley's view of sexual relations is one stripped of any ornateness, it's merely a transaction, a pleasure contract of sorts, sexual papers without the papers. In a metaphor that is both specific and general for the play, life is a card game and romance is a form of barter: Stanley expects a woman 'to lay her cards on the table' and he'll consider the offer.

What a Romantic!

Stanley's bellowing for transparency stands in stark contrast to Blanche's obfuscations, but bizarrely, in this scene, she agrees with him: 'Well, life is too full of evasions and ambiguities, I think. I like an artist who paints in strong, bold colours, primary colours. I don't like pinks and creams and I never cared for wishy-washy people'. Revisiting this after watching the play, it seems ludicrously false. Does she actually believe this? Or does she simply feed Stanley the line he expects to defuse tension? Whichever option, Stanley doesn't buy her silly flirtations for a second. He responds to her simulated simpering of 'I said to myself, 'My sister has married a man!'' with a [booming] Now let's cut the rebop!' Not only is Stanley sensitive to such playacting, he's violently allergic to it. What he wants to talk about is business. Blanche's tricks may work for the more refined men she knows around Laurel, but Stanley is clearly a completely 'different species,' as Stella says.

One of the most memorable moments in this scene is when Stanley manhandles Allan Gray's love poems. In his brutish way, he enacts his entire life philosophy in one act. His bewilderment ['What in hell are they?'] at what these poems are and their function is nigh on comical, but telling in the huge gulf between the refined Southern Romantics of Blanche's imagination [and the wider cultural imagination of the American South] and the coarse modern utilitarianism embodied by Stanley. Dealing with him may make Blanche 'faint with exhaustion' but he simply will not stop until he gets what he wants: those elusive papers, which of course, he gets, because that is what always happens. To be fair to him, he is thorough. He may not understand the jumble of legal papers but he's a man with friends and he knows someone who will.

The antagonism between them fades when she hands over the papers, but the scene delivers a classic Big Reveal moment before transitioning to Scene 3: Blanche finds out Stella is pregnant. It is striking that Stanley, rather than Stella, reveals this. It is another example of the complete control that Stanley exerts in their marriage and his dedication to laying the cards on the table. Disconcertingly, Blanche spends way more time recalling her flirting with Stanley than she does congratulating Stella on her wonderful news. It's also revealing that she contemplates that 'maybe he's what we need to mix with our blood now that we've lost Belle Reve'. Despite his brutish harassment, there is already a strong attraction between them and, certainly, Blanche notes his powerful presence and bullying ability to get what he wants. Stanley's power and magnetism excites her and she cannot help talking about it. Stella has lived her life in Blanche's shadow, and perhaps that was one of the reasons why she left Belle Reve aged 15. Though she keeps her thoughts to herself, Stella may not appreciate Blanche starting to destabilise her already tempestuous marriage.

Scene 3 is one of the most dramatic in the play and it is the payoff of Williams' careful building of tension in the previous two scenes. We know Stanley's personality is volatile, we know he's going to be drinking like a drought-hit warthog when the sisters are out, we know poker night will be a big boy's banter fest and predictably enough, we know the game will not be over when Blanche and Stella return. Williams' stage directions transform the apartment into a boys' playground full of riotous colour and blokey banter. The apartment should have a '*lurid nocturnal brilliance, the raw colours of childhood's spectrum*' which is achieved through 'the yellow linoleum of the kitchen table' lit by 'the vivid green' lamp shade. Additionally, the men's costumes create a cluster of vibrant colour blocks in the middle of the stage: their shirts are a clashing riot of 'solid blues, purple, red-and-white check, lighter green'. All of this creates a clash of colours and energies that sort of captures the chaotic energies of New Orleans itself. For the audience, it certainly presents an engaging visual spectacle, something Benedict Andrews captured in his NT production, where the poker game was soundtracked to loud rock music and the lighting was intensely lurid.

The scene begins with Stanley's animalistic slob levels set to 11. Barking orders at his pack, he tosses watermelon rinds to the floor: house proud he ain't. To amplify the volatility of the situation, his tolerance for Blanche's affected Southern manners is below zero: 'Nobody's going to get up, so don't be worried'. Drunk, he pushes the boundaries of acceptability by slapping Stella's thigh, both a chauvinistic display of bravado for his friends and an

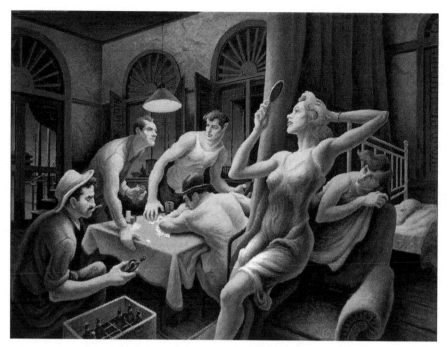

Thomas Hart Benton, *Poker Night*, 1946

objectifying gesture of possession, recalling the packet of bloody meat he
threw at Stella in Scene 1. From the off, it's clear Stanley is in a stinker of a
mood, annoyed by everyone and everything, and the tension slowly
simmers. Cleverly, Williams lowers the heat by shifting focus onto the not-so-
-cute meeting of Mitch and Blanche. Even though he 'seems - superior to the
others,' the '*awkward courtesy*' of Mitch's behaviour presages their disastrous,
stilted date in Scene 6. Williams shapes an idiolect for Mitch that is slightly
elevated above that of his peers, so it does seem that, even if it is just in terms
of his language and his more refined manners that he may possibly represent
a romantic lifeboat for Blanche.

The tiredness, the heat and the drunkenness are all swirling into a heady brew.
The scene itself is drunkenly wobbling from Stanley to Blanche and
back. However, Stanley just won't go away. Whenever the play starts to calm,
he storms back into focus, demanding silence or subservience or both. His
annoyance at the music from the radio is irrational: he is the only person on

stage irritated by it. Williams then switches back to Mitch and Blanche where he constructs a moment of connection. Mitch's bizarre waltz with Blanche is the epitome of lumbering movement. He *'moves in awkward imitation like a bear,'* and is often played for laughs. It really can be very funny indeed. However, it is this farcical action that makes the rapid ascent into domestic violence so shocking. There is a sudden switch from drunken tomfoolery to serious trauma. In a dark way, it is the pressure release the scene was calling out for, but its impact on the audience can be as violent as the slap itself. Different productions do different things: Williams' actual stage directions hide the sight of the violence, choosing to reveal it through sounds: *'there is the sound of a blow,'* Stella *'cries out'*, Blanche *'screams, 'there is grappling and cursing. Something is overturned with a crash'*. This can hide the audience from the reality of the violence, but it can also make them more imaginatively involved. In contrast, Benedict Andrews' 2014 production was full of actual physical violence, with Ben Foster smashing Vanessa Kirby full in the face, blood spurting from her nose.

Ultimately, in the structural tug-of-war between Blanche and Stanley, it is he who is stronger. Subsequently the scene follows him and his anguish, not Blanche and her budding romance. However, modern audiences are likely to be troubled by the acceptance of domestic violence as merely an added extra of passionate love. Isn't the play a little too glib in its assertions of 'There's nothing to be scared of. They're crazy about one another'? This is supposed to reassure Blanche [and the audience] but Mitch's repeated declaration that 'poker should not be played in a house with women' is more revealing of the underlying patriarchal bias of the playworld, unsubtly blaming the women for upsetting their poker game. The solution seems to be just to change the venue rather than change the behaviour. It's all irrelevant anyway as Williams seems intent on blinding the audience with the nuclear fusion of Stanley and Stella's relationship.

The violent lurch of dramatic focus from Blanche to Stanley facilitates one of the most famous scenes in all of American drama, immortalised by Elia Kazan's 1951 film version with Marlon Brando bellowing 'STELL-LAHHHHHH!' *'with heaven-splitting violence'*. It is jolting to see Stanley's anguish and vulnerability and his pleas to Eunice, 'I want my girl to come down with me!' are surprising in both their intensity but also in their neediness. It's also really surprising to see the stage direction *'humbly'* used to describe his actions.

However, his enormous anguish and the passionate reconciliation makes great, mesmeric drama. How should the audience feel about this reconciliation, though? What are we to make of Stella's sudden U-turn from 'I want to go away, I want to go away!' to '*they come together with low, animal moans*'? Sure, the sexual enthrallment is clear. It's hardly sensible behaviour though [cue exam question: Discuss!]. Have a look at how Kim Hunter plays this in Elia Kazan's 1951 film and compare it with Vanessa Kirby's interpretation in Benedict Andrews' 2014 National Theatre production. The subtle differences are fascinating.

So, like Blanche's closing observation that 'there's so much - so much confusion in the world' this scene's chaotic structure and rapid acceleration from drunken ambling to seismic sundering and on to sensual rapprochement make it one of the most vital scenes in the entire play. Beginning with Stanley's intolerance for the sister's feminine intrusion, it ends with a plea for tolerance and 'kindness'. Unfortunately, Blanche is in completely the wrong place if she's looking for this.

Scenes 4-6

Scene 4 takes place the morning after Stella and Stanley's fight. At the end of the previous scene, Blanche has seen Stella go back to Stanley, in spite of his violence towards her, Mitch reassuring her that it wasn't serious. Like Blanche, the audience is keen to know what's happened.

In order to heighten the dramatic tension, Williams employs a series of contrasts in this scene. From the beginning, there is a 'confusion of street cries' outside, while Stella, to Blanche's horror, is lying serenely in bed inside the apartment. The stage directions describe her 'almost narcotised tranquillity', suggesting the drug-like effect her physical relationship with Stanley has, and it is clear from what Stella says that, after the alcohol-fuelled aggression of the previous night, Stanley has calmed down and feels 'very, very ashamed of himself'. Although for Stella this is reason enough to forgive him, for Blanche it is unacceptable. She has been quick to brand Stella's behaviour as 'insane' and Stanley as 'a madman'. She also stands in the doorway of the apartment, looking in, further distinguishing her from her sister and indicating that, although they are related, they no longer share the same values. Stella is part of Stanley's world now. She is powerfully attracted to him and, of course, her pregnancy no doubt further cements her loyalty to her husband. Additionally, as the stage directions indicate, Blanche's appearance contrasts entirely with Stella's. This can also be seen in their behaviour: while Blanche is frantic, neurotic and, as Stella says, 'hysterical', Stella is 'calm and leisurely'. Blanche makes frequent use of interrogatives and exclamations: 'He's left?' and 'Will he be back?' or 'Baby, my baby sister!' and 'I've been half crazy, Stella!' In response, Stella begs her to 'stop yelling' and accuses her of 'making too much fuss'.

During their discussion, which at times becomes quite heated, Williams presents us with the sisters' opposing views on masculine behaviour. While Blanche claims to be appalled by the kind of male violence she has witnessed at the poker party, Stella admits that she is 'thrilled' by it. Blanche has been terrified for her sister, while Stella is strangely accepting. More than that, Stella confesses that Stanley 'smashing' the light bulbs on her wedding night excited her. She is willing to overlook his 'powder-keg' poker nights because 'people have got to tolerate each other's habits'. When Stella tells her that she loves Stanley, Blanche's response is: 'then I tremble for you'. Stella's acceptance of Stanley's aggression reflects the strength of her attraction to him, but also says something about the reality of most women's lives in the 1940s. Maybe she doesn't really feel she has much choice.

It's interesting that, in a play set at this time, Blanche is indignant about Stella 'cleaning up' after Stanley as well - is this down to her privileged, upper-class upbringing, a feeling that Stella should not be demeaned by doing the housework, or is Blanche taking a feminist stance? If it's the latter, then she never seems to recognise the hypocrisy of herself turning to another man for support. She seizes on the idea of Shep Huntleigh as a financial escape route, but Stella is adamant that she is not 'in anything she wants to get out of'. Despite being incredulous of Stella's willingness to compromise, Blanche fails to acknowledge that in lurching from one man to the next she is effectively doing the same thing. She has no means of supporting herself, having lost her inheritance and her job. As far as she is concerned, she needs to 'get hold of some money' and a Texan oil-baron seems like a promising means of achieving this. Although she claims to be 'indifferent...to money', clearly she is not. And she won't let a little thing like Shep Huntleigh being married stop her. All this, coupled with Stella's admission that Stanley holds the purse strings, 'doesn't give [her] a regular allowance' but has gifted her $10 as an apology for hitting her, reflects the hard reality of women's lives at the time in which the play is set. There is perhaps something quite unsettling about the idea of marriage being akin to a financial transaction, even in the mid-twentieth century. Later in the scene, as the critic John McCrae has suggested, Blanche alludes to going 'to bed with' Stanley as Stella's 'job', as if it is part of the deal.

The ultimate contrast in Scene 4, however, seems to be between the primitive and the civilised. Once she realises that Stella is not going to leave, Blanche acknowledges that what 'a man [like Stanley] has to offer is animal force'. In her view, Stella and Stanley's relationship is based on 'brutal desire'. As the highly symbolic noise of the train approaching outside prevents her from hearing Stanley's approach, she goes on to express her view of him 'plainly'. Not only is he 'ordinary', an indictment of his lower-class status, but he is also 'bestial' with 'an animal's habits', 'sub-human', 'ape-like' and 'a survivor of the Stone Age'. She imagines him and his male friends, gathering at the poker party, 'grunting', 'swilling' and 'gnawing' like animals, until someone 'growls' and 'snatches' and starts a fight. In contrast, she herself hankers after a gentleman, the finer things in life, such as poetry, music and what she calls 'tenderer feelings'. Imploring Stella not to 'hang back' with the 'brutes' in the dark, Blanche longs to embrace the 'new light' of civilisation. But the relationship between Stella and Stanley is always associated with darkness; Stella has claimed that there are 'things that happen between a man and a woman in the dark - that sort of make everything else seem - unimportant'. Furthermore, when they got married, Stanley literally plunged them into darkness by smashing the lightbulbs and thus heightening Stella's attraction to him. It is entirely in keeping then that as he overhears Blanche's speech, we see what the sisters cannot, Stanley 'licking his lips', ready for the kill before moving 'stealthily' into the apartment like a hunting animal. When he 'grins at' Blanche we know that she is his prey. Interestingly, in the meantime,  Stella hugs him 'fiercely', showing she has made her choice and signalling her betrayal of her sister at the end of the play.

For three of the first five scenes the short time interval between them is made explicit; succeeding scenes take place the following morning or following evening. Between the end of Scene 4 and the start of Scene 5, however, a longer amount of time must have elapsed. Blanche mentions, for instance, meeting with Mitch and allowing him to give her a good night kiss. This detail highlights the difference between stage time and narrative time and draws out attention to how Williams manages the play's time structures for various effects. Similarly, though Scene 6 takes place at a later point in the 'same night' it includes comments that suggest days, or even weeks, have elapsed since the opening scene. Mitch refers, for instance, to 'that night we parked by the lake and I kissed you' and, although the audience have not seen Mitch and Blanche together before, their relationship has developed enough for

Mitch to have told his mother about Blanche and for him to make a marriage proposal at the end of the scene.

Following Stella and Stanley's embrace at the end of the previous scene, the action in **Scene 5** switches to Blanche, 'seated in the bedroom fanning herself'. Trying in vain to cool off, she is overwrought, and her behaviour is erratic. She 'suddenly bursts into a peal of laughter' while reading over her letter and she dominates the opening dialogue in a hysterical way. Furthermore, Blanche's capacity for fantasy is suggested by the way she 'touches her throat lightly as if actually talking to Shep'. She is enacting an imaginary conversation. Indeed, the very content of the letter is a fiction: the 'continued round of entertainments, teas, cocktails and luncheons' to which she refers clearly does not happen in Elysian Fields. The lifestyle she paints for Shep is a figment of her imagination, a recreation of the privileged Southern lifestyle she has been forced to leave behind.

The tension between Blanche's fantasy world and the reality of the domestic violence going on upstairs in this scene is revealing. Offstage, Steve and Eunice are arguing furiously about another woman. Eunice is 'shrieking', there is a 'man's angry roar, shouts, and overturned furniture'. Embodying the New America into which Blanche does not fit, it is a far cry from the civilised social scene that she has been imagining. As we have mentioned before, the way Williams presents the argument is humorous - quite uncomfortable perhaps for the audience. Even Blanche, who we might expect to be shocked, light-heartedly asks whether Steve has, in fact, killed his wife. Coming hot on the heels of the fight between Stella and Stanley in Scene 3, this kind of domestic violence seems par for the course in Elysian Fields. In this raw, uncivilised environment at least, Blanche's romantic illusions are startlingly out of place. That she is an outsider is also brought to bear later in the scene. Stanley greets everyone except her and, having made up after their respective arguments, the coupling of Eunice and Steve and Stanley and Stella accentuates Blanche's 'aloneness'. While she 'sinks faintly back in her chair with her drink', Eunice 'shrieks [this time] with laughter' and Steve 'bounds' joyfully after her. Similarly, Stanley and Stella 'twine arms as they follow, laughing'. For Blanche, the alcohol on which she depends is her only company.

The juxtaposing of Steve and Eunice's short-lived fight with Stanley's confrontation of Blanche about her past is also significant. Through this, Williams explores two different kinds of 'violence' in the characters' relationships. Stanley's treatment of Blanche here is psychologically aggressive. As he talks to her, he 'jerks open the bureau...slams it shut... throws his shoes' and starts to undress again. These actions can all be interpreted as thinly veiled threats, driven no doubt by what he has overheard in the previous scene. Mercilessly he refuses to humour Blanche anymore. As she tries to assert her superiority by claiming she is 'compiling a notebook of quaint little words and phrases' from Elysian Fields, Stanley retorts: "you won't pick up nothing here you ain't heard before'. He makes it clear that he, unlike some of the men she has known, can see through her affected primness and is far from intimidated by her old Southern status. In fact, shortly afterwards, he torments her by mentioning 'somebody named Shaw', a man from her past in Laurel. Although she remains composed, 'her face expresses a faint shock' and once again she laughs 'breathlessly'. Blanche's efforts to cover up her past and deceive Stanley are neatly summed up by the stage directions: 'She speaks lightly but her voice has a note of fear'. Her game is almost up.

Once left alone with her sister again, Blanche's fear rises to the surface. She 'closes her eyes as if faint' and her hand 'trembles' as she looks around 'with an expression of almost panic'. She launches into a long justification to Stella of her promiscuous behaviour in Laurel after the loss of Belle Reve, finally admitting that she has 'run for protection...from under one leaky roof to another leaky roof'. Blanche sees herself as a victim, forced to seek shelter from a metaphorical storm of which she has been 'caught in the centre'. Reflecting perhaps the time the play is set, she identifies the need to have her 'existence admitted by someone'; to survive, she needs a man to value her: 'People don't see you - men don't...unless they're making love to you'. Losing her youthful good looks, then, is what makes her feel so 'awf'lly scared'. Blanche relies on being attractive to men to get by and, understandably, the thought of getting older makes her feel vulnerable. Stella, on the other hand, dismisses her fears as 'morbid' and feels concerned about whether Blanche is interested in Mitch for the right reasons.

Finally, and just before Mitch arrives, Blanche flirts with a young man collecting for the Evening Star newspaper, the name of which perhaps draws attention to the disparity in their ages. As an audience, we cannot fail to find her predatory behaviour both deeply unsettling and also exasperating. Blanche cannot resist doing what she knows is wrong. The boy's youth is signalled in many ways: he is shy and awkward, uncomfortable, 'bashful'. It also emerges that he has sheltered in a drug store and drunk a 'cherry soda'. This leads to Blanche's lascivious reply: 'you make my mouth water'. As he tries to escape her advances, she manically exclaims: 'Young man! Young, young, young, young - man!' and kisses him. We already know that Blanche's husband was very young; she has also lost her teaching job over an illicit relationship with a pupil. Blanche's penchant for young men has been the cause of her downfall on more than one occasion. So, when 'Mitch appears round the corner with a bunch of roses', her supposed 'Rosenkavalier', we can't help feeling that their relationship is just another fantasy.

Williams chooses not to show us Blanche's and Mitch's date. Instead, the action in **Scene 6** switches to 'about 2 a.m. the same night' after they have been to the amusement park. The mood is markedly muted - Blanche's behaviour reflects 'the utter exhaustion which only a neurasthenic personality can know', one of Williams' very particular stage directions and quite challenging for the actress playing her part. Neurasthenia, now an obsolete term for nervous anxiety, is often associated with the kind of chronic stress associated with war and perhaps provides some indication of the immense pressure on Blanche at this point in the play. Clearly, her anxiety has cast a shadow over the evening, as Mitch is described as 'stolid but depressed' and as laughing 'uneasily'.

At the beginning of the scene, both Blanche and Mitch try to accept the blame for their rather abortive 'date'. Mitch worries he hasn't shown Blanche a good enough time; Blanche, who has been unable to 'rise to the occasion', feels she has failed to fulfil her role: 'the lady must entertain the gentleman - or no dice!'. This line confirms what she has already explained to Stella: because she is so dependent on men for her security, she also feels obliged to offer something - 'entertainment' - in return. The transactional nature of this might seem shocking to a modern audience, and to the more liberated women who had successfully taken on men's roles during the war. Blanche, however, holds on to traditional gender values, in this scene adopting a rather helpless female role as she asks Mitch to find her key for her.

The conflicted nature of Blanche's personality is strikingly evident here as well. As they stand in the doorway, Blanche appears to be sending Mitch on his way, asking him how he will get home, saying 'I guess you - want to go now...'. Shortly afterwards, however, she invites him in. On the one hand, she berates Mitch for asking permission to kiss her, yet we know that she has discouraged his advances in the past and does so again at the end of Scene 9. One moment she is described as 'stopping lifelessly', the next she speaks exuberantly of creating 'joie de vivre'. The mixed messages are difficult for Mitch to decipher. At this stage in the relationship, he is, however, clearly fascinated and intrigued by her caprice, claiming that he has 'never known anyone like [her]'.

As the stage directions lead us inside the house and 'the interior walls can dimly be seen', the atmosphere becomes increasingly oppressive. Having reached for the alcohol once again, Blanche indulges in yet another fantasy, this time that she and Mitch are in an artist's cafe in Paris. What happens next is excruciating for the audience to watch: she imagines them as La Dame aux Camellias and Armand, the protagonists of Alexandre Dumas' tragic romance about an innocent young man who falls in love with a courtesan. In French, which she knows Mitch cannot understand, Blanche suggests he might like to sleep with her; then, in English, she implores him to take off his coat, which results in a humiliating discussion of Mitch's perspiration problem and his heftiness.: Awkward, forced, embarrassing, it is the opposite of romantic. When Mitch, this time in role as Samson, picks Blanche up, he tries to embrace her and once again she rejects him in the name of propriety, claiming to have 'old-fashioned ideas'. The stage directions, which tell us that 'she rolls her eyes, knowing he cannot see her face', suggest otherwise. There is, of course, a huge disparity between the image Blanche wishes to project and the reality.

Williams maintains the tension between these two 'sides' of Blanche throughout the scene. When Mitch opens up to her about his mother's imminent death and wish to see him 'settled', his candidness elicits a sympathetic response from Blanche. It also prompts her to confide in him about the circumstances of her husband's death. Perhaps it is Mitch's vulnerability and attachment to his mother that reminds her of her own semi-maternal relationship with Allan, who was 'just a boy'. Looking out of the window, as if into her memory, she recalls her first experience of love and the shocking discovery of his homosexuality. Although she never refers overtly to this, it is thinly veiled in references to Allan's 'softness and tenderness' and the fact that she wouldn't have guessed, as he did not appear 'effeminate'. During this long confession, Mitch allows Blanche to speak uninterrupted, but the sound effects of the locomotive train and the light that shines through the window create a dramatic immediacy to the story. After Blanche found Allan with another man, they tried to pretend nothing had happened, drove out to a Casino and 'danced the Varsouviana'. During the dance, Allan left the casino and killed himself. According to Blanche, 'it was because… [she'd] suddenly said "…You disgust me!"'. In an explosion of exclamations, Blanche re-enacts the scene, the responses of the other onlookers, the grim details of the suicide. She ends by telling Mitch that, since this traumatic event, the light has gone out of her life.

Finally, Mitch summons the courage to embrace Blanche, drawn to her frailty, and recognising their mutual need for somebody. Their embrace offers a transient moment of hope, embodied in Blanche's cryptic line: 'Sometimes - there's god - so quickly!' But it doesn't last long.

Scenes 7-9

For the first time since the opening scene, Williams specifies the date. The fact that it is now 'mid-September' tells us firstly that Blanche has been living with Stella and Stanley for four months and secondly that summer has given way to autumn.

Coming hot on the heels of Blanche being 'saved' by Mitch, this scene brings Stanley centre stage, as he dishes the dirt on 'Dame Blanche'. The scene is set for 'a birthday supper' which we know must be for Blanche as she referenced her forthcoming birthday in Scene 5. She also makes much of her star sign being Virgo - the virgin at this point but by **Scene 7**, Stanley is ready to reveal what we have long suspected, that Blanche is very far from being a virgin, despite her romantic ideals. This scene is one of storytelling as both Stanley and Stella offer their 'truths' about Blanche.

The scene begins with an exchange of stichomythic dialogue between Stanley and Stella while Blanche soaks, oblivious to the coming crisis, 'in a hot tub.' Although the balance of the dialogue looks very equal on the page, closer inspection reveals Stanley to be taking control of the action by his aggressive questioning. In typical curt, monosyllabic fashion Stanley asks 'What's all this stuff for?', 'She here?'.

Stella's responses always defend Blanche but stay on the right side of moderate. She doesn't rise to Stanley's mimicry of her sister and becomes increasingly monosyllabic as her own position is exposed. The snappiness of the dialogue is broken with Stanley's comparatively expansive 'And you run out an' get her cokes I suppose? And serve 'em to her majesty in the tub?' Obviously, this is what Stella *has* been doing, despite being heavily pregnant, and this adds weight to 'the dope' Stanley is about to reveal about Blanche. Stella's line, 'Stanley, stop picking on Blanche' underestimates the power that Stanley has over Blanche and the childlike, 'picking on' is a rather insipid understatement for a bitter fight for supremacy, just as her criticism of the supply man as 'mean and rotten' is utterly inadequate.

Again, Stella reminds Stanley of the 'different circumstances' of their upbringing - she doesn't attach value to it, she merely points out the difference. Nevertheless, Stanley is vehement in his reactions, 'So I been told. And told and told and told!' Again, his lack of education is evident in the ungrammatical 'I been' but the emphatic repetition of 'told' is a warning of Stanley's rising ire. Stella's loss of control over this domestic disaster is made clear in the use of dashes in 'No, I don't and -' together with 'What _ things?' She is prevented from finishing her sentences and is clearly struggling to make sense of what Stanley is telling her.

That Stanley has 'got proof' from 'reliable sources' leaves us feeling pretty queasy. What sort of man goes out of his way to victimise a woman who is obviously vulnerable? It's also telling that in his determination to expose the 'pack of lies' Blanche has been telling, he fails to realise that if he sabotages her relationship with Mitch, Blanche will have nowhere to go and she will have to stay with them. Stanley's 'noble' intentions to 'save' Mitch from Blanche's machinations justify his actions, but fail to take into account the needs of either Blanche or Mitch. We guess, really this is only a cover for Stanley getting what he wants, to destroy and be rid of Blanche.

As Stanley embarks on his narrative about Blanche's past, his account becomes more expansive and Stella's defence of her sister becomes increasingly weak. The striking thing about Stanley's condemnation of Blanche is that here is a story based on male perspectives about a vulnerable woman whose behaviour doesn't fit the norms that are deemed acceptable. She hasn't committed any crime and her misrepresentations are not intended to hurt anyone. Yet Stanley's seems to relish recounting her shady past. If he can't yet hurt Blanche directly, he gets a kick out of souring her relationship with her sister.

Stanley's enumeration of the types of infidelities experienced by Blanche is fairly predictable - she has resorted to staying at The Flamingo where her promiscuity resulted in her being 'requested to turn in her room key for good'. Her 'act' is exposed as 'downright loco - nuts' and as if Stanley needed to say more, he continues with his tale of Blanche's place being 'out of bounds' to a nearby army camp. His piece de resistance is the account of her entanglement with a seventeen-year-old boy. This revelation probably has more impact to a modern audience than at the time when the play was written. Unlike would be the case today, Blanche broke no laws, but the affair has the added impact of being catastrophic in terms of her financial security. She is declared as 'morally unfit for her position' as a teacher and effectively run out of town.

Much of the horror at Stanley's brutality here lies not in what he has to say but how he says it; he claims to deplore Blanche's 'lies' but in his retelling of her fall from grace, his euphemisms actually make the sorry saga more, not less, salacious. The point is, Stanley doesn't hate to tell Stella about her sister; he loves it, he is getting even at her. His vindictiveness is breath-taking. Calling her 'Dame Blanche,' 'royalty,' 'her Majesty' and comparing her 'fame' to 'the president of the United States' reveals his deep social insecurities, despite all his blustering bravado.

Stella's defence of Blanche is steadily eroded by Stanley's chronicle and by the interjections of 'Dame Blanche' who Williams positions carefully at this point in the play to embody all the sense of entitlement which Stanley so detests. Despite a spectacular list of Blanche's moral lapses, Stella can only respond weakly with 'she was always...flighty.' This is both inadequate and strangely apt all at the same time and that is why Blanche is so difficult for audiences to pin down. Stella admits to disapproving of some of Blanche's behaviour but goes on to reveal the circumstances about Blanche's marriage about which Stanley has been, before now, unaware.

It is clear Stella considers that this was the moment of crisis which shaped the rest of Blanche's life. She uses the expression 'killed her illusions' and goes on to employ words such as 'worshipped' and 'adored' to describe the intensity of Blanche's love for Allan. Significantly these words indicate a sexless, spiritual love, diametrically opposed to the physical obsession experienced by Stella for Stanley. Clearly Stella is searching for the right word to describe Allan when she plumps for 'degenerate.' Evidently, she could not say 'homosexual' on the 1940s stage, but nevertheless the euphemism is disappointing as Stella, the woman whose very essence is one of toleration, succumbs to the societal norms of the day and uses a pejorative term which undermines her sister's love for this 'beautiful and talented young man'. Despite the tragedy of Blanche's situation, Stanley shows no mercy. 'Her future is mapped out for her' is both threatening and untrue.

And where has Blanche been while all this has been happening? Out of sight but not out of mind in the bathroom. Her 'contrapuntal' singing of 'Paper Moon' is an uncomfortable counterpoint to the main action of the scene. The  lyrics are pure fantasy and indicate the fragility of Blanche's world. She is a 'make believe' creation but if someone 'believed' in her, it might all just come good. Even while Stanley systemically demolishes Blanche's genteel facade, we hear her 'frolicking in the tub' like a child. She 'thrusts' her head out of the door and merrily chirps 'Not so terribly long! Possess your soul in patience!' Later she emerges with a 'gay peal of laughter.' This is the most upbeat we see Blanche and all the while her destruction is happening. This is dramatic irony at its most devastating.

The denouement of the scene comes quickly. Super sensitive, Blanche realises that 'something has happened' and declares 'you're lying!' which is uncharacteristically direct. Rapidly the scene reaches fever pitch where the 'hectic breakdown' of the piano symbolises the collapse of Blanche's stability and prepares the audience for the inevitable disaster of Scene 8.

Scene 8 occurs only 45 minutes after Scene 7 and it is notable that scenes 7 - 10 all occur on the same night, giving a heightened sense of the rapidity with which Blanche hurtles towards destruction. It is also worth considering what might have happened in the gaps between the scenes.

The scene begins with a specific reference to the urban setting with the 'water tank or oil drum' set in the 'empty lot.' This industrial landscape is juxtaposed with references to light in the form of 'pinpoints of lighted windows and 'a torch of sunlight'. References to light will be picked up later in the scene with the birthday candles on the cake.

Blanche, Stella and Stanley are engaged in a 'dismal' birthday supper. The vacant fourth place is significant as we guess that Mitch hasn't shown up, thanks to Stanley's efforts. Blanche's 'tight, artificial smile' shows how hard she is trying to keep her emotions under control and the atmosphere is tense.

These efforts to control the situation are horribly exposing. She persists with her 'southern belle' act when she says 'is it because I've been stood up by my beau?' which is larded with euphemisms. Stella's feeble laugh encourages another comment from Blanche in which she admits to having 'a good deal' of 'experience with men'. Coming so soon after Stanley's revelations, this is uncomfortably near the knuckle - Blanche often undercuts her pretences with frank admissions, but here it is excruciating for the audience and for Stella.

Blanche's pathetic attempt to lift the mood with 'a funny story' draws Stanley back into the action but also gives Blanche another opportunity to display her refined sensibilities as she insists on a story which is 'amusing but not indecent'. Again, the recent revelations hover over the action. Whether Blanche deliberately goads Stanley or if she has become accustomed to disparaging him is open to question, but remarks such as 'more vulgar expressions than Mr. Kowalski!' stoke a simmering resentment that ignites when Stella finally snaps and accuses him of being 'too busy making a pig of himself.'

At this point violence erupts with Stanley hurling a plate to the floor. The intensity of the verb underlines Stanley's ferocity. Stanley sums up his issues with Blanche in a few short sentences and includes Stella in his condemnation. He accuses them of being 'a pair of queens', which reminds us of the way he described Blanche in Scene 7. His parting shot, 'Remember what Huey Long said - 'Every man is a king!' And I am the king around here so don't forget it!' expresses Stanley's admiration for a figure associated with left-wing politics is an obvious juxtaposition with the entitled upbringing of Blanche and Stella with their plantation and servants.

When Blanche and Stella are left alone together, the fight seems to have gone out of Stella. She cries 'weakly' and her responses to Blanche are feeble; 'nothing, nothing, nothing'. Her words lack any determination and she resorts to mild remarks such as 'I wish you wouldn't' when Blanche decides to call Mitch. Meanwhile, in a statement characteristic of her sense of entitlement. Blanche 'intend[s] to be given an explanation from someone.'

Blanche's attempt to telephone Mitch is another example of 'contrapuntal' action, as in Scene 7. As she makes the call, Stella and Stanley reconnect. Stella reminds us of Blanche's fragility by calling her 'the girl' and she cries 'quietly'. Stanley reminds Stella of the way it was before Blanche showed up. He is clearly talking about their sex life when he talks about getting 'the coloured lights going' during 'them nights we had together'. To underline his need for an uninhibited sex life, Steve and Eunice are overheard laughing together, unencumbered by another person in their home.

While this is going on Blanche makes the futile phone call to Mitch. She is achingly formal in her conversation with the person at the other end of the line and is left 'lost' and 'frightened' when she doesn't get through.

The birthday cake moment is significant for several reasons; normally a birthday cake has candles to show the person's age. In this case, Stella has stopped at 25 candles which only draws attention to Blanche's unwillingness to admit to her real age. Later in the scene she also claims to be 27. The white cake suggests her purity. Blanche's reluctance to light the candles is accompanied by one of her fanciful speeches, this time about the baby; 'Oh I hope candles are going to glow in his life and I hope that his eyes are going to be like candles, like two blue candles lighted in a white cake!' To some ears this expresses Blanche's poetic soul, but Stanley is scornful of such self-conscious lyricism. Ignoring him, Blanche continues with her theme and expresses her fears that 'candles burn out' and after that 'electric light bulbs go on and you see too plainly'. Clearly, she is referencing her own pain and her own desire to avoid bright light.

The scene continues with a moment of heightened emotion, this time from

Blanche when she overreacts to Stanley's complaints about the heat. She calls

him a 'Polack' again which gives Stanley another opportunity to espouse his patriotic creed; 'I am one hundred percent American, born and raised in the greatest country on earth'. Whereas Blanche is proud of her aristocratic French bloodline, Stanley is committed to rejecting his humble Polish roots and becoming part of a new America.

Stanley's control over the women is exemplified in the way he handles the phone call. Blanche jumps to the conclusion that it is Mitch calling but Stanley takes the call and discusses bowling with 'Mac'. He orders Blanche to 'keep her seat' and the phone call reveals the casual authority also Stanley holds over his team-mates. He is the 'team-captain' and refuses to bowl at 'Riley's' because he had 'a little trouble' - presumably a fight - last week. In one short phone call, Williams reminds us of Stanley's working-class life, his sense of superiority and his proletarian interests. His description of Blanche as 'a noisy woman on the place' is typically demeaning and dismissive.

The phone call seems to re-establish Stanley as 'the king around here'. This is the moment he chooses to give Blanche her 'birthday remembrance' - a bus ticket back to Laurel. This is spectacularly cruel as it mimics the 'tributes' she received from her 'admirers' in the past. When Blanche cannot believe what the gift is, Stanley callously fills in her words for her; 'Ticket! Back to Laurel! On the Greyhound! Tuesday!' Her reaction mirrors the evening of her arrival when Stanley clumsily referred to her marriage. She tries to laugh but is violently sick, as the Varsouviana swells again, symbolising her mental disintegration.

Despite the horror of the evening Stanley is determined to go bowling, as is his perceived right. Stella's criticism goes up a notch here as rather than referring to people who hurt Blanche in the past, she now includes Stanley - 'people like you abused her' - which signifies a distinct shift in her attitudes. Claiming he 'done nothing to no-one' - the double negative revealing that he has definitely done something to someone – Stanley again refers to the sex life he and Stella used to enjoy. He understands that his working-class credentials were a key part of their initial attraction, claiming to have 'pulled [Stella] down off them columns' and how [Stella] loved it.

While Stanley is banging on about their sex life, Stella goes into labour. 'Her look goes suddenly inward as if some interior voice had called her name.' She moves in a 'shuffling progress' with 'a blind look and a listening expression' which Stanley, preening himself in his bowling shirt, fails to notice. Stella's concern for the 'interior voice' arguably plants the idea that even once Blanche goes and the baby is born, things will never be the same again for Stella and Stanley. Stella's imperative 'Take me to the hospital' is quietly powerful as Stanley, for once, 'supports her'.

Left alone, Blanche emerges 'twisting a wash cloth' which connotes her fevered mind. Her refrain of 'El pain de mais' is a peculiar end to what has been a turbulent scene. She is using Spanish, one of the languages we associate with the melting pot culture of New Orleans and the reference to bread without salt suggests that the bread will go stale quickly.

Scene 9 dramatises the inevitable collapse of the romantic relationship between Blanche and Mitch, and with it, the evaporation of all the desperate hope Blanche had invested in him as her gallant rescuer. Some critics argue that it contains the true climax of the play, the tragic moment for Blanche when all her hopes are dashed and any escape route from disaster blocked off.

The action unfolds a 'while later' on the same evening as Scene 8. It is clear what Blanche has been doing in the interim; drinking to try to escape her situation. She is in a 'tense, hunched' position and the recovering of the bedroom chair adds to the pathetic effect. As with the Chinese lantern earlier in the play and the 'light cover' on the bed, Blanche has attempted to cover the reality of the apartment. No amount of soft furnishings can, however, hide the hard truth.

Throughout the first part of the scene, the Varsouviana plays, indicating Blanche's feverish thoughts. We can tell things are bad because now she 'whispers the words of the song', like a child trying to comfort herself.

Mitch arrives at Elysian Fields unshaven, inebriated and in his work clothes. In contrast, when Mitch arrives, Blanche is desperate to preserve appearances: she 'rushes about frantically' hiding the drink in a closet and dabbing her face with powder and cologne. In a last-ditch attempt to keep Mitch, she launches into a full-on southern belle routine, feigning coy reserve and using flamboyant language about his behaviour which she describes as 'So utterly uncavalier!' Following his rejection of her kiss, she is 'fearful' as Mitch 'pushes past her' and 'stalks' ominously into the bedroom.

The speech that follows from Blanche reveals her mental deterioration; she's desperate to keep the show on the road but at the same time she reveals how very unstable she is becoming with her repeated questions. The crunch comes when Blanche implies that Mitch is too insensitive [or slow-witted] to ever 'get anything awful caught in his head' and refers to him as a 'dumb angel-puss', which is hardly fitting for the lumbering Mitch.

Once again Blanche and Mitch circle each other uncertainly with the exchange about the fan. Mitch is blunt, 'I don't like fans', while Blanche elaborately tries to accommodate him; 'Then let's turn it off, honey. I'm not partial to them.' Offering Mitch a drink, Blanche slips up. In denying that she is drinking Stanley's liquor, she inadvertently reveals that the stuff is her own having already said  'I don't know what there is to drink'. When she later 'discovers' the bottle of 'Southern Cheer', she seems to have forgotten her charade, keeping up the pretence of not knowing what it is, drawing too much attention to it. Mitch is no longer fooled; he has been told by Stanley that she has been 'lapping it up all summer like a wild-cat'. This is an interesting simile - Blanche is the most refined, perhaps overly refined, of creatures, so to describe her as a wild animal shows how the men struggle to reconcile her manners with her actions.

Blanche's discordant mental state means that the Varsouviana plays for a significant proportion of the scene. She tries to explain its significance: 'The polka tune they were playing when Allan - wait!' but Mitch has little truck with what he now sees as affectation. In his newly enlightened state, his response shows none of his previous sympathy. His only recourse is to think that she must be mad; 'Are you boxed out of your mind?'

Loftily Blanche defends herself against the accusation of drinking: 'What a fantastic statement! Fantastic of him to say it, fantastic of you to repeat it! I would descend to the level of such cheap accusations to answer them, even!' However, Mitch is keen to expose the 'real' Blanche which is seen in the references to light and daytime which follow. This section operates on at least two levels; Mitch wants to see Blanche literally so he can 'take a look at [her] good and plain' and work out how old she really is. However, this harsh exposure also reveals Blanche for what she is, a hypocritical, down-at-heel, faded southern belle, with no money and suspect morals. Simultaneously, Mitch's actions reveal him to be no gallant Southern gentleman. When he turns the light on, stares at her and quickly turns the light off again, it suggests that Mitch doesn't like what he sees.

The dialogue reaches a moment of heightened honesty in this section of the scene. Blanche admits to her fabrications - 'I don't tell the truth. I tell what ought to be the truth!' while Mitch 'slowly and bitterly' confesses that he didn't mind Blanche 'being older' than what he thought, 'But all the rest of it - God!'

Scenes 10 & 11

For much of **Scene 10** the audience is made to hope that, against all the odds, Stanley's joy and pride in having a child will prove a stronger force for good than his smouldering resentments against Blanche. However, however much the audience hopes for this, we also know, absolutely, that this hope is in vain. Hence, as we watch the events unfold, we are made to endure a prolonged and terrible feeling of dread.

At the start of the scene, Blanche is shown alone in the flat. She is in a bad state. She has been drinking and has dressed herself up in crumpled white garments. Talking to herself, she imagines being taken on a 'moonlight swim' to sober herself up. We see Stanley arrive and we are told that he too has been drinking.

Initially their conversation is cordial enough. The stage directions make Stanley's habitual way of looking at Blanche less unnerving than usual; he is 'grinning *amiably*'. Then Blanche starts up with the lies. She claims to have received a telegram, from Shep Huntleigh, inviting her onto a cruise. In response, Stanley's tone sours and turns sarcastic. Then he takes off his shirt and the tension goes up a notch or two. But, it goes down again when Stanley opens the bottle and, surprisingly, offers Blanche the chance of a reconciliation: 'Shall we bury the hatchet?' Politely Blanche declines. When Stanley picks up his brilliant pyjamas the tension picks up again, though at this point, the pyjamas are as much associated with celebrating the birth of his child as with the joys of his wedding night.

For the dramatic effect to be tragic what happens in this scene must seem inevitable, unstoppable, fated, while at the same time, paradoxically, there must be some sense that alternative outcomes were possible. At this point, it seems possible that hope might triumph - that Stanley's joy in fatherhood will, indeed, trump his desire to vanquish Blanche. But then Blanche's monologue about herself shifts the balance of Stanley's mind. For one thing, she is being delusional again and describing herself in those lofty superior ways, extolling the 'beauty' of her mind and 'richness of the spirit of tenderness' of her 'heart'.

But it is the reference to 'swine' that really snags Stanley's attention, pricks his hostility and turns the atmosphere ugly. When Blanche then lies about Mitch, Stanley has had enough with her pretences, her ridiculous airs and graces, bluntly calling her out on her lies: 'There isn't no millionaire! And Mitch didn't come back'. He doesn't spare her feelings. He wants his words to hit home and to hurt.

Blanche is so taken aback that five times in a row she can only respond to his verbal attack with pathetic 'ohs'. His temper riled, he insults her, telling her to take a look at herself in her crazy get-up and he laughs at her and tells her he saw through her act right from the very start. When Stanley disappears into the bathroom, the stage directions convey viscerally Blanche's increasingly disturbed and terrified state of mind. In desperation, she tries to ring for help.

Stanley's re-emergence is both dramatic and ominous. He throws open the bathroom door and emerges in his new costume, the brilliant silk pyjamas. The self-conscious theatricality is disturbing, signalling that Stanley is now in a different state of mind, ready to perform. Now his grin has lost any traces of amiability.

There is a silence as the adversaries stare at each other. Other outcomes are still possible, just about. Then we hear the clicking of the phone. Stanley's movements become horribly self-assured. He is in full control. Putting the phone back on the hook, he blocks Blanche's escape route and grins again, as if in anticipation or triumph. We hear the locomotive and the blue piano. All thoughts about the joy of fatherhood have disappeared from Stanley's mind. Now he has other things on his plate. 'Come to think of it,' he says brutishly, 'maybe' Blanche 'wouldn't be too bad to – interfere with…'

Blanche tries to defend herself with the bottle, but, like a hunting animal, he 'springs towards her', overpowers and disarms her.

Scene 10 is the most controversial scene in the play. Unsurprisingly, when *Streetcar...* was turned into a film, the production company wanted to have it cut. Some critics object to Williams including a rape scene at all. Others have objected to Williams' treatment of sexual assault. Some critics have labelled the playwright a misogynist. Considerable critical attention has also focused on the adjective 'inert', as used to describe Blanche as Stanley carries her to the bed. Made uneasy by Blanche's lack of resistance here and sometimes keen to redeem Stanley, some critics have argued that to some extent she provoked the attack and even allowed the sexual assault to happen. This interpretation ignores her nervous hysteria, however, and the fact that she has been drinking heavily and that she is utterly exhausted. Perhaps, Williams is not suggesting Blanche doesn't want to try to fight Stanley off but that, by this point, she is entirely incapable of doing so. Certainly readings that seek to shift some of the responsibility for the rape away from Stanley and onto Blanche seem like victim blaming.

Other critics have responded to the sexual violence by trying to read it in fundamentally symbolic rather than human terms, with Stanley cast, for instance, as the masculine force or the proletarian one, and Blanche his feminine or aristocratic opposite. In these readings, Scene 10 dramatises the symbolic defeat of the female by the male and/or the old order by a new one. No doubt these symbols are present in the scene, but the power of the drama comes, surely, from the human suffering, particularly from Blanche's terrified confusion. If Williams merely wanted to convey a symbolic defeat he could have done so in myriad less disturbing, less visceral ways. Surely he wants the audience to feel Blanche's terror, to be horrified by it and feel enormous pity for her.

When **Scene 11** opens, a few weeks have passed. The buddies are assembled again to play poker. Blanche is bathing, again, trying to wash herself clean. Meanwhile Stella and Eunice discuss Blanche's confused state of mind. When she appears, timidly from the bathroom, Blanche is very specific about how she wants to dress, because she is expecting, mistakenly, her beau, Shep Huntleigh, to arrive. The dramatic irony is heart-breaking. Understandably, Blanche is nervous and reluctant to enter the room where the men are assembled, but it is a trial we know she will have to face. In short intercut mini-scenes, our attention is shifted swiftly from the rough talk of the men to the anxious preparations of Stella and Eunice and on to Blanche's 'faintly hysterical vivacity' as we wait for all three to be brought together and for Blanche to be disabused of her illusions and her desperate hopes.

After learning that Shep hasn't called, Blanche is shocked when she hears the abrasive voice of her abuser, Stanley, so close by in the kitchen. The stage directions then describe how a 'look of sorrowful perplexity as though all human experience shows on her face'. It's a horribly poignant description and quite a challenge for any actor to convey, all this emotion in just one memorable expression. It suggests that, despite appearing on the surface to be utterly bewildered, perhaps even 'crazy', at some level, Blanche senses her true predicament. Hence she asks, 'What's going on here?' This scene would be terribly sad if Williams had presented Blanche as merely mad and lost,

 unaware of what was happening when she is taken away to the asylum. However, Blanche's flickers of awareness, her immense sorrow and, later, her desperate resistance generate the emotional power of tragedy. Aristotle's term, anagnorisis, refers to the moment in a tragedy when the scales drop from the eyes of the protagonist and they discover the true nature of their circumstances. It is a moment of illumination, where the blindfold they have been wearing for the entire action of the play is finally removed. We are fast approaching this moment in Streetcar..., but Williams gives it a further agonising twist by having Blanche in a near hysterical state, half wanting to deny what she also half realises.

Because, despite her misgivings, part of her still hopes against hope that rescue will arrive. And part of her is also still bravely trying to keep up appearances, to maintain some dignity. When the doorbell rings, although she looks 'fearfully' at Stella and Eunice, and despite being able to hear the polka faintly in the background, Blanche still asks, 'Is it the gentleman I was expecting from Dallas?' That fearful look tells us that to some extent she knows it is not.

By definition, tragedies end with the death of the protagonist. But Blanche does not die. Does this mean the ending is not tragic? No, because, she suffers a symbolic death. As the cathedral bells ring in the background, funeral bells perhaps, her monologue about dying at sea makes this clear. Blanche imagines herself a romantic death scene in which she is finally purified, 'sewn up in a clean white sack… into an ocean as blue as… my first lover's eyes'. We guess the reality will be horribly less romantic.

The doctor and matron arrive and Blanche finally realises the truth. The moment of full anagnorisis has come. Seeing it in the face of the doctor, Blanche makes one last, doomed, attempt to escape her fate. Stanley is brutishly callous, Mitch pathetic, Stella and Eunice not much more than helpless bystanders. Stanley and the matron's cruel, rough treatment of Blanche ensures the audience sympathises even more with her. This is not the way such people should be treated. And then there is the last, terrible caving in of her resistance, Blanche's final exhausted acceptance of her fate in the form of the doctor's arm, before she is led off stage for the last time.

Stella may be devastated, crying out her sister's name, but it is a footnote, an afterthought, a pale echo of her sister's immense suffering. Decisively, this is Blanche's tragedy now.

Stanley acts repulsively, trying to touch into Stella's blouse. The blue piano starts up, with the muted trumpet. Guiding us exactly how not to respond to what we have all just witnessed, the other men carry on the poker game, unconcerned, as if they have seen nothing, and feel, nothing.

The end.

Except that, perhaps, there can be a more hopeful reading of the end of the play. When she exits, Blanche is dressed again in her smart clothes, a restoration, perhaps, of her appearance at the start of the play. And perhaps in the doctor she has at last found the protector she craved and can begin another life.

Blanche Dubois

Hamlet, for women

Gillian Anderson, who played Blanche in the 2014 NT production of *A Streetcar Named Desire*, likened the role to 'Hamlet, for women'. It is a useful starting point in an analysis of Williams' presentation of Blanche, not only suggesting that hers is a challenging, complex part, the pinnacle of an actress's career perhaps; but also, in associating this iconic character with Shakespeare's most celebrated tragic hero, Anderson's comment points us towards a range of opposing critical reactions, rooted as they inevitably are in their own historical contexts, to Blanche's character as it evolves throughout the play.

Like many of literature's most compelling female characters, Blanche elicits a variety of often conflicting responses from audiences too. On the one hand appealing in her vulnerability and fascinating in her audacity, she is melodramatic, attention seeking, snobbish, vain. Blanche might remind us a bit of Curley's wife in John Steinbeck's *Of Mice and Men*, at once a vulnerable woman, the victim of a cruelly patriarchal society, yet at the same time provocative, dangerous and sometimes contemptible in her treatment of others. Blanche is a pleasingly real character, though: she is flawed and credible, and audiences cannot help but be intrigued and captivated by her.

Arguably, for Tennessee Williams, Blanche was the main attraction. Close to calling the play *The Moth*, Williams frequently presents Blanche as 'moth-like' in her appearance, movement and love-hate relationship with the light. What do audiences associate with moths? Mystery, a kind of dusty beauty, vulnerability, perhaps death - a paradoxical mix of characteristics which suggest that Blanche is both attractive and repellent, alluring yet dangerous. Unsurprisingly, Blanche has been the subject of a range of feminist readings. What is surprising, however, is how often they differ. Does Williams himself condemn Blanche as the disruptor of happy marriage, a needy, self-centred, delusional interloper, who drives a wedge between husband and wife and, moreover, the heartless villain who precipitated her husband's suicide; or does he wish audiences to empathise with her as the tragic victim of a brutal patriarchal society or, indeed, celebrate her as a powerful female figure who is both ready and willing to challenge the patriarchal forces that seek to oppress her?

At the beginning, she doesn't seem like a powerful figure. Passively delivered by the streetcar of the title, Blanche arrives in New Orleans in a state of diffidence and confusion: she looks at a slip of paper, then at the building, then again at the slip of paper and so on. She is in 'shocked disbelief' at the squalor she finds in her sister's new neighbourhood. Even the way she is dressed is 'incongruous' in this environment. As her name and all her bathing suggests, she likes to project a refined, chaste image, but with this comes a fragility, signalled by stage directions such as 'daintily', 'delicate' and 'startled'. Fergus Parnaby suggests, 'she is already at the end of her 'journey' by the time the play begins' as she arrives in the final resting place of the gods, Elysian Fields.

Although Williams presents Blanche as a credible character in herself, she clearly has symbolic value as well, representing the uncomfortable shift in power from the Southern aristocracy to new, urban industrialists in the early twentieth century. Her first interaction is with Eunice, who asks her if she is 'lost'. This is a significant question, which can be interpreted on several levels, not just geographical. Everything about Blanche's demeanour reflects a lack of direction and stability - from her helpless adherence to what 'they told me' to her heavily hyphenated, disjointed speech patterns. Blanche is already 'on the edge' when she arrives; she does not know where or who she is. By the end of the play, therefore, we can't help feeling that she had been on a tragic trajectory from the very start.

Secrets and lies

Blanche is a woman with secrets, which undoubtedly accounts for much of her strange and furtive behaviour. She claims she 'rarely touches' alcohol, yet she clearly depends on it, stealing it from the cupboard before Stella has even returned home. Although her name might suggest moral purity and innocence, she is in fact extremely duplicitous. Right from the start she tries to cover up her past: the reasons for her arriving unexpectedly at Stella's house, why she has lost her job, what has caused the death of her young husband. She hides her face from bright lights, dissembles and indulges in fantasy, candidly revealing to Mitch in Scene 9, 'I'll tell you what I want. Magic! Yes, yes, magic! I try to give that to people... I don't tell the truth. I tell what ought to be the truth.' This desire for magic can be interpreted in more or less sympathetic ways. Cate Blanchett, who played her in Liv Ullman's 2009 production, suggests that the 'flame of inspiration that Blanche represents - that fragile, ephemeral poetry - is extinguished'. This elevates Blanche to something much more positive than the destructive threat to post-war domestic ideals she comes to signify in other readings.

In plays we often learn a lot about characters from other characters, and clearly Stella and Stanley have quite opposing views of Blanche. Stella tries to insulate her, keeping her away from the poker party, fearing 'how she'll take it'. Similarly, she tries in vain to manage Stanley's behaviour towards Blanche, warning him not to mention her pregnancy and suggesting that he compliment her appearance. Maybe Stella is not just protecting her sister, though. Perhaps she is reluctant for Stanley to get to know her. He may not be well-educated or upper class, but he is quick to see through his sister-in-law's pretensions. Crucially, when Blanche claims not to understand what 'ideas' he might have about her, he exclaims: 'Don't play so dumb. You know what!'. While Blanche dresses herself as 'a cultivated woman...of intelligence and breeding', Stanley mercilessly strips her back down to what she really is.

In scene 2, the interaction between Stanley and Blanche prepares us for events in scene 10. After one of her many baths, Blanche wears a 'red satin robe' and flirts 'playfully' with her sister's husband, asking him to button up her dress. There is a dangerous attraction between them, which Stanley acknowledges just before he rapes her, when he claims 'we've had this date with each other from the beginning!' There is also a great deal of power play going on between them in the earlier scene. Clearly, Blanche cannot assert herself in a physical way over Stanley. She therefore tries to use her sexuality and also her superior command of language, 'fancy' words such as 'peruse' instead of 'read' and references to literature, to gain the upper hand. What plays out subsequently is a battle between Blanche and Stanley for Stella's affection. And Stanley wins.

When, in the next scene, Blanche and Stella arrive home after a night out to find Stanley's poker game still in progress, Blanche's first concern is her appearance and how she will be perceived by the men. Retreating quickly to the bathroom, her sanctuary, she claims her 'nerves are in knots'. It is at this point that she meets Stanley's friend Mitch for the first time. Blanche's interest is sparked immediately as Mitch seems 'superior to the others' and, as such, might be the knight in shining armour who can rescue her. The danger signs are all too clear, however, as Blanche assumes a persona that she thinks will impress Mitch, lying first of all about her tolerance for alcohol, then about her age and also about her reasons for visiting her sister. The scene ends ominously with a violent, alcohol fuelled argument in which Stanley throws the radio out of the window and attacks Stella. This is one of the play's many disquieting moments, but what is also interesting is the reaction of Blanche, who is quick to pass judgement on Stanley's behaviour as 'lunacy', a chilling portent of her own fate at the end of the play.

Similarly, Blanche's hostile response to Stella and Stanley making up after their fight signals her downfall. With a typical lack of self-awareness, she regards

Stella's capitulation, her forgiveness of Stanley, as 'insane' and claims that Stanley is a 'madman'. Coming from Blanche, maybe this is a bit rich and, immediately afterwards, Williams presents Blanche herself leaping into a fantasy about escaping with 'Shep Huntleigh', whom some critics suggest may even be a figment of her imagination. While in the role as Blanche, Gillian Anderson claimed that she felt 'like [she] was hanging on to reality by a thread'. As the play progresses, Blanche's grip on reality certainly becomes looser and looser and she starts to slip up. Not knowing that Stanley is eavesdropping outside, and perhaps not acknowledging her own 'wild' side either, she seals her fate by insulting him as 'common' and 'bestial'. Her attempts to convince Stella to leave him because he is 'an animal' and 'sub-human', 'ape-like' - the list goes on - are all overheard by Stanley himself and give rise to his need to eliminate her. Blanche is a threat to his relationship with Stella. She criticises his neighbourhood, his class and his home. Hugging Stella closely, in a scene full of dramatic irony, he menacingly 'grins through the curtains at Blanche'. The gloves are off.

A tragic reckoning?

The beginning of Blanche's inevitable, tragic undoing comes immediately after this scene when Stanley reveals what he knows about her past. After losing the family home, Blanche has had various physical relationships with different men in Laurel; as a 1940s 'Southern Belle', she is ashamed and afraid that she will be found out. In a long speech to Stella, she argues that women need to use their sexuality to get by. But, although she regrets her promiscuous behaviour, she is nevertheless unable to prevent herself flirting with [particularly young] men, as demonstrated by her interaction with the boy collecting for the Evening Star newspaper. She seems irresistibly drawn to him, like a moth to a flame, calling him 'honey lamb', kissing him and then berating herself 'to be good and keep [her] hands off young children'. All this after she has just told Stella how anxious she is to earn the respect of Mitch. The audience could, at this point, be forgiven for feeling that Blanche is her own worst enemy. Liv Ullman, who directed the 2009 production, controversially claimed that 'there are no bad people in this play; they just do bad things to each other'. Her sentiments echo those of the playwright. Writing to Elia Kazan, the director of the 1951 film, Williams said, 'there are no 'good' or 'bad' people' in the play. It's difficult to see Stanley in this light, but while Blanche might not be a 'bad' person, she certainly does many 'bad things', not least to herself.

Not surprisingly, Blanche's duplicity and her past eventually catch up with her and, warned off by Stanley, Mitch rejects her, shockingly condemning her as 'not clean enough to bring in the house with [his] mother'. Soon after, Stanley rapes Blanche while Stella is in hospital giving birth. Directorially, this scene has been handled in a variety of ways, leading to considerable debate about how compliant Blanche actually is and the extent of her part in her own demise. There is no doubt, however, that with the ominous 'inhuman voices like cries in a jungle' and 'shadows and lurid reflections' on the wall, coupled with the seediness of French Quarter life going on outside the apartment, it is a bleak and pessimistic moment, which some critics have seen as the real climax of the play. Afterwards, Stanley arranges for Blanche to be taken to a psychiatric hospital and Stella reluctantly agrees as, encouraged by Eunice, she has chosen not to accept Blanche's 'story' of the rape. Both sisters, it seems, have a capacity for self-delusion, which they use to survive. In the final scene, Blanche exits, 'lead' by the doctor 'as if she were blind'. Like many of the characters in this play, she has failed to know even herself and eventually succumbs once more to 'the kindness of strangers' in the only way she knows how.

Does Blanche have the stature of a tragic hero like Hamlet? Not all critics have thought so. Indeed, some have condemned her as an immoral liar and seen her as the villain of the play. However, it seems clear from reading and watching the play, and from the rest of Williams' oeuvre, that he wants us to empathise with Blanche and to find her demise tragic. In the same letter to Kazan, the playwright wrote that the play is a 'tragedy with the classic aim of producing a catharsis of pity and terror' and in order for that to happen, 'Blanche must finally have the understanding and compassion of the audience'. Can Blanche be played less as the inevitable victim of patriarchy and more as a heroic, defiant figure? Perhaps. It all depends on the production.

Stanley Kowalski

An all-American hero

Stanley Kowalski is an all-American hero. It's as simple as that. A man who has served his country with great distinction as 'a Master Sergeant in the Engineers' Corps, he came through the hellish battle of Salerno 'where 4 out of 5 wouldn't make it through'. He's put his life on the line to preserve the American way of life and he deserves some respect in 1947 from the people he's saved. He's tired of being seen as a reductive stereotype when he is 'a one hundred percent American, born in the greatest country on earth and proud as hell of it'. So, it's little wonder he takes offence at the condescending snobbishness of an extravagantly self-indulgent, self-deluding parasite from a jaded Southern dynasty. Even though Stanley knows he was 'common as dirt' it doesn't mean that he's not allowed to outgrow his origins. After all, marrying Stella is a small way of expanding his horizons, of shedding the stigmatised 'Polack' heritage that holds him back. Stella is smart: she knows that 'Stanley's the only one of his crowd that's likely to get anywhere'. She sees the future, whereas Blanche can only see the past, a fantasy place where men like Stanley have no status or power. Stanley's a futurist and he only journeys forward. He's got no time for nostalgic hankering after a romanticised past. Even Blanche admits that men like Stanley are needed to reinvigorate their faded family line, and by extension, the established land-owning gentry: 'Maybe he's what we need to mix with our blood now that we've lost Belle Reve.'

It's not just fading Southern dynasties that require re-energising, it's men like Stanley who have rejuvenated America itself, supplying the immigrant energy and innovation required to transform the U.S.A. from a 19th Century political backwater into a true 20th Century global superpower, a beacon of freedom, opportunity and democracy. And future American greatness will be built by dynamos like Stanley. A self-made man, scrabbling to the top of his potential, he's an  embodiment of the great American Dream and a representative of a new, better, more vibrant and virile America. Using his natural smarts and his persuasive forcefulness he gets what he wants and what he deserves. His name 'Stanley Kowalski' is a combination of 'stony field' and 'blacksmith'. Whimsical Blanche DuBois, aka Dame 'White Woods', flouncing about in Belle Reve, comes from another world. Stanley is a man who knows the hardship of stony fields and the hard work of smithing, he knows the poverty and persistence but yet also the achievement and success of becoming 'the king around here', the Huey Long of Elysian Fields. This is a man who can create a better future for himself and his family. Furthermore, Stanley served in the 'Engineers' Corps', meaning he's a builder, a repairman, a problem-solver. He's a Kowalski, a blacksmith, and every community needs these industrious people to grow and prosper. Stanley solves problems with the type of clear-headedness and cold logic needed to pinpoint the exact source of the issue and deduce the most efficient solutions. A man's man, he's got the contacts to find out the truth Blanche is hiding, whether it be through Shaw, 'the supply-man down at the plant' or 'that lawyer acquaintance' who can 'study out' that jumble of legal papers Blanche has hidden in her trunk.

Stanley's treatment of Blanche isn't personal; it's just basic domestic economics. His salary at the plant, which involves him being on the road a lot, is barely enough for his growing family - he's going to have a new son to provide for, after all. It's bad enough that he can't give Stella 'a regular allowance [because] he likes to pay the bills himself' but what he cannot support is a liquor-swilling, self-deluding, high-falutin' leisure lady who contributes nothing but idle notions, irritating flirtations and a lot of loose morals. And that's not even taking into account the practical annoyance of her cramping his living space and taking all those long baths - the man can't even get into his own bathroom and the apartment is sweltering enough without all that unnecessary steam. His energy bills must be all the way through Eunice and Steve's roof! Despite all this, Stanley's awareness of the Napoleonic code and his demand for a bill of sale is completely justified. He needs that money to provide for his family and Stella is owed something from that 'place in the country, the place with the columns'. Wouldn't he be an uncaring and ineffectual husband if he didn't do the things for Stella that she can't do herself? She's blinded by sisterly history to know any better, but Stanley can see straight through Blanche's lies and evasions.

Stanley is a bastion of truth, truth told pure and simple. Sure, sometimes his articulation of it can be a little insensitive, but the truth is always told. Like a private investigator, Stanley methodically goes about the mysterious case of 'The Inexplicable Loss of a Huge Plantation Mansion' with great resourcefulness, until he establishes the real goings-on up in Laurel. He simply presents his findings to the sisters and protects his best friend Mitch from a potentially disastrous marriage. Both Mitch and Stella need to know the harsh truth. Otherwise, they're just being manipulated by a duplicitous opportunist, who's 'been feeding [them] a pack of lies'. Stanley had to reveal that Blanche had been 'practically told by the mayor to get out of town' due to her outrageous promiscuity because she pretends to Mitch that she's some sort of untouched 'lily'. What's even more shocking is that Blanche has lost her source of income as a teacher because 'she'd gotten mixed-up with a seventeen-year-old boy,' which may explain her infatuation with the young man who makes her 'mouth water' in Scene 5. It's no wonder that Stella feels 'sick' after hearing this and that Mitch is sickened by the fact that she's 'not clean enough to bring in the house with [his] mother'. Like when he was a soldier in the war, Stanley's duty is to protect his 'best friend' and his beloved by defeating an enemy. It's a selfless thing he does.

Sub-human brute

It's a shame that Stanley takes such sadistic joy in doing all this. Yes, Blanche did all these things, and yes, she lied about them but, of course, she would: it's 1947, a period when hypocritical sexual double-standards of white patriarchal America ostracised a woman for participating in consensual sex. However, hard we try to see things from his point of view, a modern audience cannot forgive Stanley for his violent sexual abuse of Blanche, even though, worryingly, the early audiences of 1947 sometimes cheered as she was 'taught a valuable lesson'. Stanley's euphemistic 'rough-house' is so abusive and disturbingly quasi-incestuous that the audience cannot condone such behaviour - any sympathy we had for him must evaporate instantly. Before Scene 10, it was possible, perhaps, to side with Stanley against Blanche's delusions of grandeur and condescending attitude to him. But this is a step far too far. Stanley's sexual violence reveals he really is the 'sub-human,' 'ape-like' brute that Blanche warned Stella about in Scene 4. At that point in the play, Blanche's tirade against him seemed mere snobbery. In Scene 10, Blanche's appeal that 'in this dark march towards whatever it is we're approaching...*Don't - don't hang back with the brutes!*' becomes grimly prophetic. Earlier, her hostility seemed part of Blanche's hyperbolic hysteria, but now we realise that she sensed more than we did, that Williams distracted us with the raw sexual magnetism of the man. Blanche's fears were made look ridiculous in the face of Stella's sexual subjugation as well as her own ridiculous vanities and self-delusions. But in Scene 10, Williams reveals the hideous, violent heart of a war-like man, who rails against everything and everyone. Friedrich Nietzsche doesn't get it quite right when he declares that 'under conditions of peace the warlike man sets upon himself' - Stanley reveals the fallacy of Nietzsche's thinking: warlike men turn on those weaker than them. His vanquishing of the weaker types around him is hardly impressive: rather than an aspirational man of dynamism, he's just a small-minded, hateful bully.

What is Williams up to here? The rape is an horrific climax to his play, perturbing and incomprehensible, but why choose this action? Firstly, it acts as a catalyst for Blanche's rapid mental collapse, her moth-like delicacy finally crushed beneath the wheels of indifference and sadism. Secondly, it must turn the audience against Stanley, proving him to be the monstrous antagonist and transforming Blanche into a tragic heroine, whose suffering exceeds her crimes, a figure of pathos who provokes an audience's sympathy. Finally, the playwright provokes the audience, trying to evoke a visceral emotional response. Symbolically, Williams stated to the film censor Joseph Breen that the rape of Blanche 'is a ravishment of the tender, the sensitive, the delicate by the savage and brutal forces in modern society'. The way Williams dramatises the rape hides the actual violence from the audience, like Stanley's assault on Stella, and becomes a form of 'self-censorship', according to Bess Rowen, who also argues that the tragedy of 'Blanche's 'crime' is in having become a victim of an event that no one can bear to be confronted with every day'.

Smouldering sadist

Tennessee Williams' stage directions emphasise Stanley's virility: the man exudes a sexual charge that makes women do strange things. Just looking at the dynamic verbs used to describe Stanley reveals a maelstrom of 'smouldering' masculine energy: Variously he 'jerks', 'stalks', 'hurls', 'gives a  lough whack', 'pulls', 'kicks', 'seizes', 'slams', 'shoves', 'snatches', 'rips', 'lurches', 'tosses', 'jumps', 'bellows', 'charges after', 'advances', 'like a baying hound'. Other words describe him moving 'stealthily', laughing 'harshly', 'bawling', 'ripping off', 'pounding'. One sister rejects her high-born heritage by 'casting [her] pearls before swine' and the other sister flirts openly with her brother-in-law ['Yes - I was flirting with your husband, Stella!'], despite her sister offering the only refuge she has available. Both women act in reckless, self-destructive ways and seem helpless in the face of Stanley's sexual potency. Despite Blanche promising to 'laugh in your face' if Stella claims it's 'one of those mysterious electric things between people', the play makes clear that sexual desire and satisfaction of that desire 'sort of make everything else seem unimportant'. It's important to note Stella's enthrallment to her husband because a] it's so rarely expressed on stage and b] it seems to rob her of her agency as a woman, reducing her to crying 'on his lap like a baby' when he is away. Bess Rowen notes that the 'one of the most unnerving aspects of A Streetcar Named Desire comes from the fact that the audience and reader are meant to desire a character who is not morally sound'. While Stanley's ability to get 'them coloured lights going' seems dangerously thrilling, ultimately, he's a coarse chauvinist. Right from the start of the play he treats women as mere sexual objects: *'he sizes women up at a glance, with sexual classifications, crude images flashing into his mind and determining the way he smiles at them'*.

Alongside his capacity to make buddies, in terms of his conquering of females sexually, Stanley's a [patriarchal] man's man. But his powerful allure also makes him a woman's man, and probably also a gay man's man, a bold Williams fantasy made theatrical flesh. Rowen discusses the shocked reactions of audiences to Williams' bold depictions of sexual attraction on the stage: 'it is telling that one reaction to women being attracted to a handsome man was disbelief - implying that only a gay man would imagine that a *man* could be

an object of sexual desire'. So, Williams' brave inversion of the conventional male-subject-desires-female-sex-object dynamic felt very alien to the conservative audiences America in 1947 and well beyond. The troubling cocktail of attraction and danger was also compounded by the casting of Marlon Brando: the very first onstage Stanley and the ultimate celluloid version. Brando, who seems the closest to Williams' vision of Stanley, presents a Stanley illuminated by his own star charisma but uneasy within his own volatile personality. He is intoxicating on screen and dangerously so because he almost allows some audience members to side with him. It's a close shave but as the play's action develops Williams' works hard to maximise our sympathy for Blanche and to distance us from Stanley. At the play's end we watch Stanley's *'fingers find the opening of her blouse'* trying yet again to mask the trauma of Stella's abandonment of her sister with the fireworks of lovemaking. His problem-solving appears naïve and inappropriate - Stella may be able to lie to herself, disbelieving Blanche's accusations of rape, but it doesn't mean that she can just forget her sister completely. To complicate Stanley's voluptuous promise, he is a serial wife-beater and when he beats her in Scene 3, it is important to bear in mind that she is pregnant. Eunice roars at him in Scene 3: 'I hope they do haul you in and turn the firehose on you, same as last time!' to make clear to us that this violence is a regular occurrence. Kirsten Shepherd-Barr argues that the promise of husband and wife being able to 'make noise in the night the way we used to and get the coloured lights going with nobody's sister behind the curtain to hear' is a poisoned chalice as 'the more intense the sex, the more prone to violence the couples are'.

Notwithstanding the despicable rape of his own sister-in-law, which makes a mockery of his love for his wife, there is a cruelty to Stanley's relentless pursuit of triumphalism that is frightening. It's one thing to suspect that Blanche is feeding them a load of old baloney but it's quite another to harass her and 'grin' at her, licking his lips like a predator. It's not as if Stella hasn't asked him to go easy on her sister: 'Blanche is sensitive and [...] grew up under very different circumstances.' Stella speaks for any decent audience member when she accuses him of being 'stupid and horrid'. While 'horrid' may be a little quaint for what Stanley does, the point is that it has been made clear to him that his behaviour is unacceptable. He just chooses to ignore it as any bully would. Stanley's 'birthday present' of the bus ticket back to Laurel is a cheap, degrading shot. It's the cruel behaviour of an immature teenage boy, and an unkind boy, at that. Stanley doesn't know how to be kind, and like his name, his heart is a stony field. Williams castigates Stanley for this, in a way, because Blanche's plea for 'the kindness of strangers' is presented as a crucial moral message: if people were kinder to each other, the world would be a much better, happier place. Williams stated that his plays were a dramatisation of 'the crying, almost screaming, need of a great worldwide human effort to know ourselves and each other a great deal better'. Naive, hippyish idealism or not, he's got a point. But ultimately, Stanley wins, brutes win, men win.

Stella

Stella for star

Stella Kowalski is often seen by critics and audiences alike as merely a bridge between Blanche and Stanley. To a certain extent this is true; she is the reason why Blanche comes to New Orleans and because of this, Blanche is forced into the company of the toxically masculine Stanley. Structurally Stella forms a vital part of the unholy triangle which is formed when Blanche arrives at the ironically named Elysian Fields.

Stella's position is unenviable both as a character and for the actor who plays her. For the actor, this is probably not the role they want. Blanche is the character who gives the performer all the bravura opportunities and the more muted character of Stella is, by contrast, much more moderate in emotional range and, as a result, can often be overlooked or treated as a minor character. Such treatment, however, would do Williams' characterisation an injustice. It is Stella who brings Blanche and Stanley into the same orbit and it is Stella who tries to keep a lid on their hostilities until the night of the rape, after which Stella who is given the impossible dilemma of choosing between her sister [and the old, outdated values of Belle Reve] and her husband [and the rough reality of working-class existence]. It is Stella who we see in the last moments of the play sobbing uncontrollably, while cradling her baby.

We first meet Stella shortly after Blanche's arrival at Elysian Fields. Stella is absent because she is watching Stanley bowling. This is significant because it is Stanley who is exerting himself physically whilst Stella takes on the passive role of spectator. Clearly the men 'do things' in this environment while the women stand around and admire their masculinity. It is also our first indication that Stella has come to terms with this rough, working-class lifestyle. It seems unlikely that the young men of Stella's gilded youth would have enjoyed such proletarian pastimes.

On arrival, Blanche asks Eunice for directions to her sister 'Miss Stella DuBois, I mean Mrs. Stanley Kowalski.' This slip reminds us of the journey Stella has made from her upbringing in the refined, rarefied but impoverished Belle Reve to a two-roomed apartment in a low-rent part of New Orleans. Stella [meaning 'star'] is heavily ironic as there is little that is 'stary' about Stella.

Although she admits to enjoying bridge, which links her to the fanciful story told by Blanche as she looks up at the night sky for the Pleiades 'coming home from their little bridge party', it is significant that we never see Stella playing this card game. Her more active and sophisticated days, it seems, are in the past. Poker is the card game she now experiences, passively watching as her husband and his rough-hewn associates play it while getting drunk.

Stella is resolutely down-to-earth and the incongruity of her name is further emphasised by Blanche's dreadful nickname for her. 'Stella for star' is rendered ridiculous, even comically ironic, by its overblown poetic wistfulness. The fact that Blanche refers to her as Mrs *Stanley* Kowalski shows Blanche as a stickler for social correctness but for modern audiences, it suggests that Stella's identity has been subsumed by her husband's. The contrast between Stella's two surnames is also telling. As Blanche rather nauseatingly affirms later in the play, DuBois means 'of the woods', but Stella has taken leave of her rural past and embraced urban life. 'Kowalski' is an interesting choice of name as it has its roots in manual labour [metal working] and has come to mean 'an average person' in Polish, as we might use 'John Smith' in English. Stella is, then, established very early in the play as having her feet planted firmly on the ground. She has made her life with Stanley and seems to accept the reduction in her social circumstances without complaint.

A tale of two sisters

Quickly in scene 1, Williams makes clear the nature of Stella's relationship with Blanche. While Blanche compares Stella's 'living conditions' to Poe's 'ghoul-haunted woodland of Weir', Stella responds with pragmatic matter-of-factness: 'No honey, those are the L & N tracks'. Stella has no truck with Blanche's literary flights of fancy and this can be seen in some of the adverbs which describe her responses. She pours a drink 'carefully' and answers Blanche 'drily', both of which suggest a character who keeps a tight hold on herself and on reality. Stella is also described as 'sincere' in this section of the play which is an indication of her genuine character. Later, when Eunice goes to get a drink after her bust up with Steve, Stella describes the action as 'practical'. She doesn't judge the casual violence of the incident and her realism provides a sharp contrast to Blanche's artistic sensibilities and inflexible attitudes.

The weight of the dialogue in scene 1 is also significant. Blanche has the most lines and makes a point of saying how 'quiet' Stella is. Stella's response, 'You never did give me a chance to say much...I just got into the habit of being quiet around you,' instantly gives the audience an insight into the uneven dynamic between the two sisters. We understand how Blanche's flamboyance and loquaciousness may have overshadowed Stella and it isn't beyond the realms of possibility that this may have prompted Stella's departure from Belle Reve 'the summer Dad died and you left home'.

Blanche's criticism of Stella culminates in the lurid extended speech about the loss of Belle Reve. Hurt, Stella retreats to the bathroom. Stella's response to Blanche's dramatic monologue is wholly human and her tears, so soon after Blanche's arrival, reinforce our understanding that Stella is not insensitive - she clearly feels guilt about leaving Belle Reve - but that practical considerations are uppermost in her thinking; 'The best I could do was make my own living'. Whatever that living was [and it seems likely it may have been something to do with the war effort], Stella's new life brought her into the orbit of Stanley and, as was typical of the time post WW2, she is not in paid employment after her marriage. This leaves her financially dependent on Stanley who 'likes to pay bills himself'. When Stella is given $10 by Stanley after he has hit her and had sex with her, she immediately offers to share it with Blanche. Unlike Blanche, Stella is honest and generous with what little she has.

As the play unfolds, we also see how quickly and easily their relationship falls into a distinct pattern whereby Blanche plays the lady and Stella assumes a domestic, servile role, as if she is Blanche's maid. Frequently we see Stella performing small menial tasks at her sister's polite bequest, such as fetching her drinks or passing her towels. That this is a habitual pattern in their relationship is indicated by Stella's admission that she likes to 'wait on' her sister because it 'makes it seems more like home'. And, indeed, Stella is similarly willingly subservient to Stanley. While we might admire Stella's keenness to help her sister, for a modern readership, in particular, it is hard to identify fully with a character so willing to demean herself in this way.

Stella is caught between her loyalties to her husband and to her sister, and to what each of them embodies and Williams dramatizes this through the way that she speaks. Though her speech patterns often echo those of Stanley and the working-class characters around her, traces of Stella's privileged upbringing can sometimes be heard, particularly when she is in conversation with Blanche. When Blanche alludes to her departure from her teaching post, for instance, Stella says 'I thought you would volunteer that information', an elaborate way of saying 'I thought you would tell me'. The closest we see Stella come to breaking point is on the night of Blanche's birthday when she finally snaps at Stanley who has wrecked the possibility of Blanche leaving the apartment to marry Mitch. In a rare moment of heightened emotion, Stella bursts out with 'Your face and fingers are disgustingly greasy. Go and wash up and then help me clear the table.' Here the imperative form and the adverb 'disgustingly' convey a real sense of Stella's revulsion at Stanley's cruelty, but her words also carry a whiff of aristocratic disdain.

Clearly, Stella has some characteristics likely to endear her to the audience. Unlike her sister, and despite her upbringing, she is not snobbish or racist, for example. Married to a working-class man of Polish-descent, she knocks along happily with her working-class neighbours. Whereas Blanche is all flighty deception, Stella is practical, down-to-earth, honest and reliable. On the other hand, her willingness to be servile, both to her sister and husband, seems to be born out of a weakness and meekness of character. A similar weakness is exhibited in her tolerance of her husband's violence.

Love is the drug

For modern audiences, the issue of domestic violence is difficult to rationalise. Both Stella and Blanche fall victim to Stanley's violence and for both, sex is the outcome of violence. In Stella's case, the poker night culminates in passionate sex, despite Stanley having lashed out at her physically. Stella is in thrall to Stanley and he to her and it is significant that at the end of Scene three their reconciliation is wordless. As Stella goes on to say in Scene 4, 'there are things that happen between a man and a woman in the dark - that make everything else seem - unimportant'. Here the simplicity of her words combined with the use of dashes show how ill-equipped  Stella is to explain the deep physical connection she has with Stanley. Blanche dismisses this as 'brutal desire'. In contrast with Blanche's determination to be 'wooed' by her 'beaux', despite her promiscuity, Stella has dispensed with such niceties.

Even though we might feel uneasy and condemnatory about a sex life so inextricably linked with violence, Stella's description of being 'thrilled' by Stanley 'smashing the lightbulbs' with her wedding slipper, has a dynamism about it which is far more invigorating than Mitch stiffly presenting Blanche with flowers. The effect of a night of passion with Stanley is vividly presented in the stage directions in Williams' description of Stella having a 'narcotized tranquillity'. Stanley is like a drug to Stella and the references to Orientalism - Stella's look recalling 'Eastern Idols' - in Scene 4 suggest not only the source of those narcotics but also a rejection of Western social and sexual 'appearances' in favour of something more vital. Even though Blanche implores her to remember 'such things as art - as poetry and music,' Stanley's return from 'getting the car greased' sees Stella embrace him 'fiercely'. His smile at Blanche is a declaration of war and the territory is Stella. Although

Blanche's chances of success seem remote as Stella is not in something she wants 'to get out of.'

That Stella is pregnant is also taboo breaking. Sex with a pregnant woman might have been considered an unfit topic for the stage but the symbolism of the child is clear [and is discussed elsewhere in this guide] in terms of the mixing of the blood of the old South and the urban working class. The child is symbolic of the fertility of the union between Stella and Stanley; their relationship creates new life which is stark contrast to the fleeting encounters between Blanche and her clients. However, the gender of the child might be considered as a sign that Stanley's 'blood' has triumphed and the future of this child and the society he will inhabit will reject outdated social hierarchies and embrace the rise of the proletariat. Thomas P. Adler has stated that: 'Just as the plantation served as a symbol of the past, Stanley and Stella's baby stands for the way the 'working class's ethos will be carried into the future'.[9] As Blanche presciently remarks 'maybe he's what we need to mix with our blood now that [...] we have to go on without Belle Reve to protect us.'

Furthermore, some might see the birth of the child as another tie which binds Stella to Stanley and certainly the final scene reiterates the physical connection between the two as Stanley's fingers 'find the opening of her blouse.' Stella sobs 'luxuriously' in harmony with the 'swelling music of the blue' piano and this leaves the audience feeling far from optimistic about Stella's future happiness.

In the Elia Kazan film, the ending is more equivocal. The film censors felt that the rapist must be punished. Instead of the intimate reconnection Stella says 'Don't you ever touch me again.' She picks up the baby, starts to go in, changes her mind, says 'I'm not going back in there again, not this time, never going back, never' and leaves, running to the flat upstairs to Eunice. This ending, however, is less about Stella's self-determination and far more to do with the conventions of Hollywood's code of conduct.

---

[9] Adler, A reader's guide to essential criticism.

Far from being an 'also ran' in the narrative of *Streetcar...*, the character of Stella offers lucid contrast and strange comparison to Blanche. Blanche is itinerant, promiscuous, hypocritical and a remnant of a society which is way past its sell-by-date. Stella is married, happily some of the time, has a child, has been assimilated by New Orleans and, although her home is a far cry from Belle Reve, it is a roof over her head. However, one can argue that despite those differences, both women have made the journey from Belle Reve to New Orleans, both have relied on men to support them and both fall victim to Stanley's sexual impulses.

For many viewers, Stella's will to survive is admirable. But for others, her situation is less straightforward than it might have been for audiences when the play was published. Her willingness to 'put up with' the brutality of her husband and to be a dutiful, subservient wife is difficult to condone, while the betrayal of her sister, forcing her to live in an asylum, is also deeply problematic. For audiences in the 1940s, Blanche's promiscuity would have been reason enough to doubt her sanity and this would have made Stella's decision to believe Stanley less troublesome. In modern times, Stella's collusion with the patriarchy is harder to justify or forgive, all of which contributes to Stella being more than a simple foil to Blanche's fey idiosyncrasies.

Mitch

A gallant rescuer?

We can read Mitch's character in several different ways, depending on which and whose perspective we take. Up until the point he turns on her and decides she is not good enough to be his wife, Blanche thinks she spies a greater sensitivity and capacity for kindness in Mitch than in his rougher, wolfish friends. His male friends, however, see Mitch in a different, less flattering light. At times he is a weak, comical figure for them - they josh him and make him the butt of their jokes, and in the play's final scene, Mitch's feelings and his half-hearted attempts to intervene to prevent the removal of Blanche are dismissed, especially by Stanley, with utter contempt. Thinking about the narrative roles Blanche and Stanley allot him, brings these differences into sharpest focus: Despite her awareness of his ill-fittingness for the part, desperately Blanche tries to cast Mitch as her gallant gentleman beau, her rescuer and protector from the vagaries of life. In contrast, Stanley fears his friend might be cast in the role of the gull, a character whose foolishness is exploited by a cleverer, more devious one. As an audience, we can, of course, also adopt an independent perspective and make our own minds up about his character, and his role, from the evidence of our eyes and ears.

At first it doesn't seem impossible that Mitch could be shaped by Blanche into a gallant rescuer. If you close one eye and don't look too closely, he seems to have some potential for the role. In his initial reaction to meeting Blanche, for instance, unlike Stanley, Mitch behaves with 'courtesy', politely asking her 'how do you do' and calling her 'Miss Dubois'. Noticing his shyness and embarrassment, immediately Blanche identifies Mitch as 'superior to the others' and as having a 'sort of sensitive look' about him. Then there's the fact that he looks after his elderly mother, which suggests a caring and tender side to his nature, and he also carries a cigarette case given to him by a dead lover, inside which is a poetic inscription. That sounds a promising detail for a potential romantic lead.

Mitch also seems to be aware of how the men come across to Blanche, commenting that they must seem a 'pretty rough bunch'. Moreover, when Blanche fishes for a compliment, saying 'I'm an old maid school-teacher', he dutifully picks up the cue, gallantly replying that although she may have been a school-teacher she certainly isn't an 'old maid'. Despite the ruckus created by Stanley's violent drunkenness and the ribbing of his friends, Mitch also persists in talking with Blanche and their first meeting ends with them sitting together alone, outside of the flat, smoking and talking. In order for the eventual collapse of Blanche's hopes in him to be as dramatic and poignant as possible, it's important that the audience can believe, albeit against the odds, that for the first two thirds of the play there is some chance that Blanche might be able to shape Mitch into a dashing rescuer.

Like a dancing bear

There also early warning signs, however, that Blanche is seriously miscasting the rather limited, rather lumpen Mitch as a potential dashing 'Rosenkavalier' and that her attempts to finesse him into this role are doomed. He may greet her with courtesy, but the stage directions describe his behaviour as not smooth or polished, but as 'awkward'. His conversations with her are also limited – if they were dancing, Mitch would just be doggedly following her lead. And when Blanche does actually begin to waltz around, Mitch is described as trying to 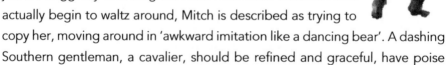 copy her, moving around in 'awkward imitation like a dancing bear'. A dashing Southern gentleman, a cavalier, should be refined and graceful, have poise and impeccable manners. Though he might mean well, Mitch is awkward and ungainly, and as the cruel, but telling, simile suggests, even rather ridiculous and comical. Although he may not be a 'wolf', we should also keep in mind that bears can be dangerous. Mitch is also all far too easily dazzled by Blanche's apparent refinement, betraying a lack of sophistication and potentially casing him in the comical role of dupe or gull. So, it seems that his friends' estimation of him might be more realistic than Blanche's fanciful one. When we next see Mitch, he is arriving to take Blanche out on their first date. Dutifully he has brought her a bunch or roses. Blanche, though, has to direct him on how he should behave, instructing him to bow to her first and then to present the flowers to her. His romantic potential is most seriously undercut though by William's use of dramatic irony: Mitch is unaware that between their first and second meeting, Blanche has been thinking of writing to Shep Huntleigh. Nor does he know what the audience has just witnessed - Blanche flirting with and kissing the young man. These details blow another hole in his credibility as Blanche's rescuer and the irony working against Mitch is again cruel, casting him, again, in a comical light.

Of course, Blanche tries to suppress her reservations about Mitch. She always struggles to distinguish between fantasy and reality and she is also in an increasingly desperate situation, so she has to squash any doubts. However, though the allusion passes Mitch by, her choice to call him her 'Rosenkavalier' is significant. Firstly, the term comes from a comic opera by Richard Strauss. Secondly, the narrative of the opera, which includes an extra-marital affair between an aristocratic woman and a seventeen year old young man, resonates uncomfortably with that of *Streetcar*.... Calling Mitch her Rosenkavalier is like a Freudian slip, it betrays something Blanche was trying to cover up, her doubts about whether he can really be her saviour.

A fumbling heavyweight

In their one whole scene together, Scene 6, it becomes more and more apparent how ill-suited Mitch is to the role Blanche has ascribed to him. Despite the heat, he doggedly wears his heavy, alpaca overcoat, not even taking it off when they sit down together. The heaviness of the coat is matched by the heaviness of Mitch's physique. Rather than being light and nimble,

Mitch's conversation is both clumsy and heavy-footed: Telling a potential lover that you're 'ashamed' of the 'way you perspire' is not a prime example of sparkling repartee or of seductive charm. When Blanche tries to make light of this unromantic bodily detail, Mitch doesn't take the hint, but continues doggedly on to describe his problems with sweatiness. Moments later, when he lifts Blanche he tries to embrace her, but does so 'fumblingly' and has to be reprimanded. During this scene, a clumsy sort of heaviness emerges as one of Mitch's most distinguishing features.

Nevertheless, though he may not cut it as the debonair, romantic figure Blanche craves, at this stage the audience may feel there is still some hope for their relationship. Perhaps Mitch could love Blanche and provide the protection for her she needs. He might be clumsy, unrefined and rather unsophisticated, but he might be good-hearted, solid, decent and faithful. Only when Stanley tells him about Blanche's past do we see another more brutish, far less likeable, side to Mitch.

From the moment he enters the flat in Scene 9, Mitch's ugly manner gives off a palpable sense of danger for Blanche. From his rough appearance and brusqueness, it is immediately obvious that Mitch 'has had a few drinks'. The following conversation reveals how he has been stewing on how Blanche deceived him and he offers only short, curt responses to her anxiously bright chatter. His tone is harsh, accusatory, embittered. Things, we realise, could very easily turn ugly.

When Mitch 'rises and follows' Blanche 'purposefully' and 'places his hands on her waist and tries to turn her about' and, 'fumbling', tries to 'embrace her', we fear that he is going to try to force himself on her. Even at this crisis point, Blanche offers him an honourable way out, crying: 'Marry me, Mitch!'. His response is shockingly brutal: 'You're not clean enough'. When Blanche threatens to shout 'fire' to get rid of him, Mitch responds with what we now understand to be characteristic heavy, slow-wittedness. He cannot seem to process what is happening and just 'stares at her', and 'still remains staring', even after she repeats the threat. Finally, he exits ignominiously as the stage directions describe him clattering down the steps. Once again, Williams uses the same adverb to describe Mitch's movement here, 'awkwardly'. From the dancing to this exit, it has become one of Mitch's signature words.

Awkward, heavy, clumsy, fumbling, potentially comical, potentially brutish, it is hard to retain any real sympathy for Mitch. The last time we see him, he also cuts a pathetic, defeated figure. His attempts to obstruct the removal of Blanche are brief and wholly ineffective: Stanley 'pushes him aside', scornfully telling him to 'Quit the blubber!', as if he is a child. Mitch then 'lunges and strikes at Stanley' who tells the others to 'hold this bone-headed cry baby!' In response, Mitch collapses on the table, 'sobbing'. Clearly this isn't the behaviour of the dashing, gallant hero, the knight of the rose Blanche so desperately wished Mitch to be.

As a character, Mitch fulfils several important roles: A friend of Stanley, he is also a stolid foil whose presence in the play highlights Stanley's more

powerful, dynamic and wolfish character. He is also Blanche's love interest and a potential saviour figure. However, he is also a comic character, through both his obvious ill-fittingness for the role Blanche has allotted him and through, potentially, being fooled into marriage by her. As long as Blanche could maintain an aura of fantasy, Mitch's inadequacies were obscured. However, in the harsh light of the day, Mitch was never up to the gallant saviour task. In the harsh light of the day, in fact, the brutal truth is that he was never even close.

Secondary characters

Eunice Hubbel

Eunice is the character Blanche meets first when she arrives at Elysian Fields, with her valise and piece of paper. In their initial interactions, Eunice is kindly and helpful, showing Blanche to the flat where Stella lives, though Blanche is rather stand-offish. Eunice lives in the flat above, but also owns the building and hence has a key to it. This detail informs us that Stanley and Stella are renting their home from Eunice and her husband Steve.

While Eunice seems to be a natural in this environment and mixes easily with the other urban characters, such as the negro woman with whom she's talking, country-bred Blanche is awkwardly out-of-place. Partly Blanche's unfriendliness may be excused by her tiredness after her journey, but it also seems to stem from social snobbery. Although the stage directions don't tell us that Eunice is working class, her speech patterns do. 'What number you lookin' for?' she asks Blanche and then tells her 'You don't have to look no further'. Blanche certainly picks up these small linguistic social markers and her stiff reactions hint at her upbringing among the Southern gentry and the prejudices she has inherited from it.

At the end of the play, loyal to her friend, Eunice helps Stella to remove Blanche from the flat and have her taken to an asylum, in part by deceiving Blanche about what is really going on. In this scene, Eunice expresses views that imply she is a stoical realist, with a particularly unsentimental view of men: she calls them 'callous things with no feelings'. She also encourages Stella not to believe Blanche's story about the rape, justifying this because 'Life has to go on'.

As a couple, Eunice and Steve's relationship provides a foil for Stanley and Stella's. As the action unfolds on-stage in Scene 5, in the background we hear snippets of argument between the couple. Eunice accuses her husband of flirting with and potentially committing infidelity with 'that blonde', an accusation he vehemently denies; 'That's a damn lie'. There appears to be an establishment on the floor above the Four Deuces bar and Eunice claims to have seen Steve 'chasing' the blond woman 'round the balcony'. The nature of this establishment is suggested by the fact that Eunice threatens to call the vice squad. Clearly the implication is that the blond woman might be a prostitute, adding to the sense of sordidness and shame involved.

Their argument soon escalates and turns violent. Eunice throws something at her husband. We hear Eunice 'shrieking'. There is a 'clatter' as something metallic strikes a wall. Steve 'roars'. Furniture is overturned. Then there's a crash followed by silence.

This scene could have been written as a grim piece of social realism, exposing domestic abuse. Instead, the fact that it all happens off-stage and we only hear, not see the action, gives it a knockabout, almost slapstick comic quality. The reactions of the on-stage audience, Blanche and Stella, are used to guide ours. 'Brightly', Blanche comments 'Did he *kill* her?' and, after Eunice's brief appearance in a state of 'daemonic disorder' threatening to call the cops, the two sisters just 'laugh lightly'. Instead of going to the police, Eunice heads for the Four Deuces to get a drink, a decision Stella immediately endorses: 'That's much more practical!'. Steve then enters 'nursing a bruise on his forehead' and sets off after his wife.

Later the same day, when afternoon has turned to early evening, Stanley returns to the flat with some drinks and yells a greeting to the flat above. His yell is met by 'joyous calls from above'. Moments later we see Eunice running down the steps, shrieking again, but this time with 'laughter', pursued by Steve who 'bounds after her with goat-like screeches and chases her around the corner'. Witnessing this, Stanley and Stella 'twine arms' and 'follow, laughing'. It seems Steve and Eunice's marital dispute was short-lived and that they have already more than made-up.

Is Williams' making light of domestic abuse? Perhaps. He seems to be showing that this sort of coarse, unrefined behaviour is both normal and accepted in this environment. It's the sort of roughhouse behaviour that is the opposite to the polite good manners expected from well brought up people in the South. But it has an earthy, sexual energy and bold vitality to it, qualities that the effete Southern sensibility seemed, in this period at least, to lack.

Eunice and Steve's dispute, and its super quick resolution, provides a frame from which to judge similar rough behaviour between Stella and Stanley. The potential, however, for this earthy, sexual energy and vitality to spill over and become cruel and destructive is always there, uncomfortably in the background.

In summary, in many ways Eunice represents the opposite to Blanche. She comes from a different class, she is urban and she is tough. Moreover, whereas Blanche is flighty and believes in fantasy, gallantry and literary romance, Eunice is practical and unsentimental, a down-to-earth realist. An additional dramatic function she performs is the parallel between her marriage and Stella's.

Steve Hubbel

An ordinary Joe, Steve is one of Stanley's buddies, his work mate, bowling partner and fellow poker player. Married to Eunice, Steve lives with her in the flat above the Kowalskis.

During the poker game in Scene 3 he tells a racist and sexual joke, indicating both his rough and ready, unrefined character and the undercurrent of racism that endures beneath the seemingly easy mixing of cultures in New Orleans. With the other men, in the same scene, he forces Stanley into the shower when he turns violent and then gets out of the flat as quickly as possible.

Steve's reactions to Stanley's behaviour signal the norms and values of his society. The fact that even Steve sometimes protests and intercedes shows just how excessive Stanley's actions can be. But, though he witnesses Stanley's violence, it doesn't affect Steve's affection for his friend. Stanley's domestic violence is tolerated and accepted by Steve and his other friends as part of the ordinary rough and tumble of life. After all, as we've already established, he has his own violent argument with his wife over a possible affair, but this blows over quickly and they are soon reconciled.

A similar pattern emerges in the play's final scene. Although Steve is shocked enough by Stanley's cruel treatment of Blanche to protest – 'This is no way to do it. She should've been told' – and jumps up from the table when he hears Blanche shrieking with terror, he doesn't actually do anything to stop what's going on. And moments after, once Blanche has been led off by the doctor and Stella is left crying uncontrollably, Steve just carries on regardless with the poker game: 'This game is seven-card stud'. Clearly this line reflects his priorities.

Pablo

As his name indicates, being either of Spanish or perhaps Mexican origin, Pablo is an example of the cosmopolitan, racially mixed nature of New Orleans. He could be second generation American, like Stanley. He is also part of Stanley's band of brothers who meet up and play competitive men's games, such as poker. Like the others, he wears a kind of uniform for the poker, a coloured shirt, and like the others he is defined by being both manly and as 'coarse and direct and powerful'. Like Steve, he is another example of an ordinary Joe, an everyman, and both characters are dismissed by Stella as never going to make much of themselves. Like Steve, during the poker night, he's more tolerant of Blanche playing her music than Stanley is and with Steve he manages to force Stanley into the shower to sober up.

Pablo only appears in the two poker games. In the second he speaks Spanish and is admonished by Stanley, 'Put it in English, greaseball' exemplifying the rough and ready, uncultured manner of the men's talk. The way that Steve and Pablo react to the Kowalskis' treatment of Blanche, signals that even these tough, unsophisticated men recognise it is appalling, and thus through them, Williams directs the audience's sympathies. Pablo comments simply that 'This is a very bad thing', before being driven back to curse in Spanish, 'Madre de Dios!' and then repeat 'mala, muy, muy mala!' [bad, very, very bad!]

The negro woman

Obviously the presence of this black character in the opening scene is intended to indicate the racially integrated nature of New Orleans. Reading the play today, we need to remember that the U.S.A. was a racially segregated country up until the 1960s and that even in liberal New Orleans desegregation didn't start until the first years of that decade. In particular, most of the South of America was still deeply divided along racial lines. Hence the inclusion of this woman in the colourful and diverse opening scene of the play and her friendly interactions with the various white characters can be seen as progressive.

It seems she's a near neighbour of the Kowalskis and a friend of Eunice's. She is present, albeit in the background, when Blanche arrives and talks with Eunice. Nothing in the script indicates how Blanche reacts to the presence of this black character, but on-stage we might expect there to be some reserve and stiffness between them as Blanche sees herself as a Southern Belle and romanticises the values and mores of the deep South.

In Scene 5, this character is briefly mentioned, just before Blanche meets the young man. She is described as 'cackling hysterically' and, though it is only early evening, as 'swaying drunkenly' as she makes her way home from the Four Deuces. Briefly she interacts with a young man heading in the other direction. She 'snaps her fingers before his belt' and then says 'Hey! Sugar!'. We can't hear what she says next, as she says 'something indistinguishable. But his reaction is telling. The young man 'shakes his head violently' and then 'edges hastily up the steps'.

What do you make of this interaction? As we know from the various cuts made to the 1951 film version, Williams had to be careful when he was dealing with taboo subjects. So his choice to make the woman's words inaudible at this precise point suggest the covering up of problematic content. It certainly seems that the woman might be propositioning the young man, either out of desire or to serve more commercial interests. Either way, this little scene adds to the impression that there are darker, seedier, more tawdry aspects to the neighbourhood.

The negro woman reappears in the play for a last time in Scene 10. When Blanche rings for help, fearing what Stanley might do to her, the back walls of the flat become transparent and a sordid scene of urban crime and opportunism is revealed. After the prostitute has been chased off by the policeman, the negro woman picks up the former's sequinned bag and starts 'rooting excitedly' through it.

From a modern perspective, Williams' presentation of this character plays into racial stereotypes and is demeaning. Firstly, of course, the woman is defined by her race and not given the dignity of a name, though, defending Williams it could be argued neither are several other characters, such as the young man and the sailor. Secondly, she waits patiently in the background when the two white women are talking in Scene 1 and then performs a task for them, like a servant. Moreover, she is twice shown to be involved with unwholesome, possibly criminal, activities, first seeming to solicit a young man and then to steal from the prostitute's bag.

The young man

In Scene 5, a young man comes to the flat to collect money for the newspaper, the Evening Star. Alone in the flat, Blanche is preparing herself for her date with Mitch, who she has just told her sister she wants to be with 'very badly'

 and who she sees as her rescuer and protector. However, Blanche cannot stop herself from flirting with the young man. She makes him come over to her and light her cigarette and when the obviously discombobulated young man backs away from her, she follows him, moving seductively 'close' to him, speaking 'softly to him'. When he reveals he has been drinking a cherry soda at the drug-store, Blanche is shockingly immodest and frank about her sexual attraction to him: 'You make my mouth water'. Although the young man is described as feeling uncomfortable and as 'bashful' as a 'kid', Blanche continues to behave in a

151

predatory, seductive manner, ordering him to 'Come here! Come on over here like I told you'. Then, 'without waiting for him to accept, she crosses quickly to him and presses her lips to his', kissing him. After dismissing him, even more shockingly she tells him she's 'got to be good and keep my hands off children'. We have to remember here that she was employed as a school teacher.

The interaction with the young man reveals Blanche's irresistible and transgressive attraction to youth and the trouble she has trying to control her erotic desires. Depending a little on the age of the actor cast to play this character, the exploitative and sexually predatory nature of the interaction is likely to distance the audience from Blanche, with a modern audience, in particular likely to be appalled by such behaviour.

Some critics have suggested that Blanche preys on young men like a vampire in an attempt to recapture her lost youth and vitality. Less Gothically, Roxanna Stuart, an actor who played Blanche several times, thought that the young men's 'innocence and purity were cleansing for her' or that 'that they reminded her of Allan Grey, her young husband who killed himself'. However when she suggested this theory to Williams, the playwright rejected the idea, saying that 'in her mind she has become Allan. She acts out her fantasy of how Allan would have approached a young boy'.[10]

As we have already mentioned, earlier in the same scene, the young man seems to have been propositioned by the negro woman. So he has two interactions with older women in short succession, both of whom treat him sexually. The close repetition of similar predatory behaviour suggests that this might be a common experience for the young in the world of the play, and recalls the difficulties Blanche's husband, the play's other young man, had navigating his way through a harsh, often unsavoury and sometimes predatory world.

---

[10] Roxanna Stuart, *The Southernmost Desire.*

The doctor

Tellingly, the cast list introduces the doctor as 'a strange man'. And this, indeed, is Blanche's first impression of him when he arrives in the play's final scene. The stage directions indicate his 'unmistakable aura of the state institution' and Blanche seems to pick this aura up immediately. She had been expecting her rescuer, Shep, so when the doctor arrives and first speaks to her she is so shocked that she gasps and runs back into the flat. However, after the matron has forced Blanche outside, the doctor removes his hat, crouches down, as one might to a child, and speaks to Blanche in a gentler, more reassuring and respectful tone. And this change in manner calms Blanche. Rather than resist, now she 'extends her hands towards' him and allows herself to be drawn up 'gently' and supported. While the doctor leads her out of the flat, Blanche is 'holding tight to his arm'.

Blanche's interactions with the doctor are significant in several ways. Firstly, they reflect how easily a woman could be confined to a medical institution at this time. There appears to have been no diagnosis or any attempt at treatment before Blanche is taken off, presumably, to an asylum. Thus, it seems disturbingly easy for Stella and Stanley to have Blanche committed. And it also seems like revenge, a punishment Stanley meets out on Blanche for telling Stella about the rape and a way of disposing of her. It's a tragic betrayal too if Stella has her sister incarcerated because she didn't believe her story.

The change in Blanche's attitude to the doctor once he removes his hat also shows her keenness to submit to male authority and her desire to find male protection, that elusive cleft in the rock of the world. Once she reads his behaviour as showing gallantry, Blanche thinks of the doctor as a gentleman rescuer. This dependency on a man is a weakness Blanche has inherited from her upbringing and exposes how she is constitutionally unable to escape the chivalric codes of the deep South.

It is difficult to tell whether this change of behaviour was a strategy used by the doctor or whether it suggests he will continue to treat Blanche's with kindness and respect once she's incarcerated in the medical institution.

The matron

Williams' presentation of the matron encourages the audience to side with and feel sympathy for Blanche. When she tries to extract Blanche from the flat, for example, the stage directions describe the matron in the way that Blanche perceives her, as a 'peculiarly sinister figure'. We have already been told that the matron shares the doctor's aura of 'cynical detachment'. Unlike like him, however, the matron doesn't try to charm Blanche or soothe her obvious distress. Speaking to Blanche in clipped, curt phrases, the matron is brisk, no-nonsense and business-like. Showing zero empathy for her patient, who is terrified and crying out and screaming, the matron physically restrains Blanche and then manhandles her out of the flat. Described as heavily built, the matron is also heavy-handed. At no point does the she consider that her harsh way of treating Blanche is making her more distraught. Bluntly, she asks the doctor whether Blanche should be put in a straight-jacket, like a madwoman. If the doctor's behaviour provides some hope that Blanche might be treated kindly in the future, the matron's rough physicality, her 'lack of all the softer properties of womanhood', combined with her utter lack of empathy, provide a sobering and chilling corrective to this.

If we read the play as being about how a patriarchal society punishes a woman who deviates from acceptable social norms, as Blanche does by being promiscuous, then, like Eunice and Stella, the Matron illustrates how women can conspire to uphold and maintain patriarchal power.

The street vendors

At the start of the play, a street vendor is selling food and we him or her shouting 'Red hot! Red Hot!' Partly, of course, Williams uses the vendor to create the sense of an urban street scene, with the vendor's voice one of four characters that speak a series of short lines in quick succession. But a vendor could have been selling any kind of food, with the appropriate accompanying street cry. The choice of the phrase 'red hot' is clearly significant, not least because it is repeated four times here and then again when the vendor re-enters the play at the end of Scene 2. The connotations of 'red hot' are multiple, but the main effect is to establish an atmosphere of heated desires.

Scene 9 is another short two-hander in which Blanche's potentially romantic and redemptive relationship with Mitch comes to its unhappy climax. As Mitch becomes more aggressive and his tone bitter and accusatory, Blanche is forced to try to defend herself. As things get heated, the play's second street vendor enters, a 'blind Mexican woman in a dark shawls' carrying 'gaudy tin flowers' of the sort displayed at funerals. Like the negro woman, her presence in the play confirms the racial mix of New Orleans. Additionally, that she is blind and selling cheap tin flowers suggests she is impoverished. In this way, alongside the drunk and the prostitute we see briefly in Scene 10, she helps convey to the grimy roughness of this quarter of New Orleans. The stage directions tell us that her 'calling is barely' audible and her 'figure is only faintly visible'. Making eerie, 'soft mournful cries' she is like a ghost, or a prefigurement of death. Her association with death is further cemented by her repeated cry of 'Flores, flores para los muertos' [flowers, flowers for the dead].

The sailor

The unnamed sailor is part of the confusing mish-mash of voices in the street scene with which the play opens. He is trying to find a bar, the Four Deuces, which will be mentioned intermittently during the action. The negro woman warns him that the bar is a 'clip joint', i.e. a place that overcharges its customers, maybe a place of ill-repute or a fleshpot. The fact that the sailor has a date at the bar connects alcohol consumption and sex. This connection is further implied through street vendor's cries of 'Re-e-ed h-o-o-ts!' Thus the sailor's short contribution to the dialogue helps establish the play's atmosphere of intoxication and desire.

Stella and Stanley's baby

Throughout the play, the South and the North, the old America and the new, as embodied by Blanche and Stanley, have been in perpetual conflict. In the baby the Dubois blood of the French-influenced South will mix with the Polish Northern blood of the Kowalskis. Hence, the couple's baby signals hope that in the future these conflicts between the Old gentrified South and the new, proletariat North may be settled, and a new integrated American identity be born.

Off-stage characters

Allan Grey

In Scene 6 we learn about the young man Blanche married when she was only sixteen and his tragic suicide. Blanche tells Mitch that 'there was something different' about Allan, a 'nervousness, a softness and tenderness that wasn't like a man's', sensitive features that remind us, of course, of Blanche herself. Like Blanche, Allan also sought protection from the abrasiveness of the world, turning to and marrying Blanche, desperately seeking 'help': 'He was in the quicksands, clutching at me.'

Soon after they were married, Blanche discovered Allan in bed with another person. Later in the play we learn that this other person was male, confirming the earlier suggestions that Allan was gay. After the discovery, the three got drunk at a casino, where, on the dance floor, Blanche told Allan that 'you disgust me'. Allan then ran outside and moments later a gunshot was heard.

So, like Blanche, Allan was a tender, sensitive and delicate soul who struggled to cope with the brutality of the modern world. Like her, he also had a huge secret to hide - his homosexually. Blanche also associates Allan with a bright light that illuminates the world. Later, in Scene 7, we learn from Stella, that Allan was 'extremely good-looking', that he 'wrote poetry' and that Blanche didn't 'just love him but worshipped the ground he walked on'. To Blanche, Allan seemed to embody all the qualities she most admired in humans so she 'adored him and thought him almost too fine to be human'.

The kind of struggles a young gay man would have had growing up in America at a time when homosexuality was criminalised are indicated by the way Stella categorises this 'beautiful and talented' young man as both corrupt and immoral, as a 'degenerate', because of his homosexuality. Tellingly, the 1951 film version erases Allan's homosexuality entirely, with Blanche's scorn for her husband triggered instead by him being 'weak'.

Shep Huntleigh

When she is desperately trying to think of ways for Stella and herself to escape in Scene 4, Blanche decides to write to a fabulously rich ex-boyfriend, Shep Huntleigh, only to abandon the plan almost immediately. According to her, Blanche had a relationship with Shep when they were college students and came across him again during her holiday to Miami, where she was trying to catch a millionaire. Blanche tells her sister that, having run into him accidentally, she got into Shep's Cadillac convertible. We don't hear what happened after that, but we do learn that Shep is a married man.

Obviously, Blanche is not the most reliable of narrators. At best, she has a tendency to romanticise the truth, stretching it longer than Shep's Cadillac.

So, we have to read between the lines here. Thinking of herself as a Southern Belle, Blanche presents Shep in the corresponding role of her beau, a gentleman rescuer for a damsel in distress, or, as she calls Mitch, a potentially protective 'cleft in the rock of the world'. We might assume that the meeting was innocent. However, there is the mystery of the source of Blanche's extravagant wardrobe. Revelations later in the play about Blanche's recent past at the Flamingo Hotel also suggest that her meeting with Shep might have been less than innocent: she may have had a fling or affair with a married man or, worse, have been paid for her affections.

Williams uses Shep to reveal further dimensions to Blanche and her back story. As we noted in her reactions to the doctor, it is characteristic of her, for example, to imagine she needs a gallant male rescuer to help her escape any predicament because she doesn't consider she has the capacity to rescue herself. As we know, Blanche often struggles to distinguish between fantasy and reality and is prone to lying. While she tries to maintain the impression that her relationship with Shep, if there is one, is of belle and beau, the reality might well be far less romantic.

Near the end of the play, in Scene 10, Blanche tells Stanley that Shep has telegrammed her an invite to a 'cruise of the Caribbean on a yacht', providing a way for her to escape from her increasingly fraught situation in the flat. That this is another fantasy is indicated both by Blanche's agitated state and by Stanley's obvious disbelief. In the following scene, Blanche's references to Shep have changed, however, in a fundamental way. Up until this point in the play, at some level, Blanche seems to be aware that she is lying or fantasising or dressing the truth up a bit. This time, despite the complete lack of evidence and despite the fact we repeatedly see her fail to contact him, she is completely convinced that Shep will ride to her rescue. This change indicates a dangerous shift in the balance of her mind: tragically, she seems to be losing her grip on reality.

Hence in Scene 11, she is bewildered when Stella tells her she hasn't had a call from Shep. When the doctor and nurse ring the bell, she asks hopefully whether it is the gentleman she was 'expecting from Dallas'. The doctor enters, Blanche 'gasps', retreats into the flat and speaks in a 'frightened whisper', saying 'that man isn't Shep Huntleigh'. Her desperate belief that she will be rescued at the last minute, and by Shep, adds to the acute poignancy of the play's final scene.

When life becomes too difficult to face, sometimes people create an alternative fantasy world. Over time, they can come to believe in this fantasy world, developing delusions about the nature of reality. It is entirely possible that some, or even all, of Blanche's stories about Shep Huntleigh are part of her fantasy world. In the most extreme case, Shep Huntleigh was just a figment of her imagination and never existed in the world of the play. In a less extreme reading, it is the relationship between Blanche and Shep that is the fantasy.

Critical reception & productions

The critical reception of the play has changed over time, as cultural materialist critics would expect, with each context of production foregrounding slightly different aspects of the play, but it always comes back to the Blanche-Stanley dynamic. Bess Rowen observes that the general trend in productions 'is to cast an actor who is over 40 but still youthful, beautiful and vivacious to play Blanche alongside actors not known for brute force or uncontrollable sexuality as Stanley.'[11] It is a remarkably enduring play with numerous American and international productions since 1947. The most notable recent production was directed by Rebecca Frecknall in 2023 and starred Irish actor, Paul Mescal, as Stanley. Frecknall's vision of the play saw a return closer to Williams' original Stanley, with 27-year-old Mescal delivering a performance of 'fierce and dangerous energy'.[12] Other reviews noted the innovative use of sound and music in this production, something that would have delighted Williams.

For the sake of brevity, this section will limit its focus to the first Broadway production and subsequent 1951 film, both directed by Elia Kazan, and Benedict Andrews' 2014 production for the National Theatre. The logic is simple. Both of these are easily available to watch in their entirety. Kazan's 1951 film is widely available to stream online or watch on DVD and Andrews' production can be rented via the NTHome website. Minor diversions will be made to other productions to explore more unusual or noteworthy approaches to the play.

Initial Reception

On its initial Broadway production in December 1947, the play was both lauded and criticised. However, despite some mixed reviews, the overall impression was favourable: it was a Broadway smash running for 855

---

[11] Bess Rowen, Introduction to *A Streetcar Named Desire*.

[12] Arifa Akbar, *Guardian*, January 2023.

performances and won Williams a Pulitzer Prize in the process. Together with Arthur Miller, Williams' plays were seen as reinvigorating American theatre after World War Two, staging more risk-taking and visceral drama. *Streetcar...* was certainly thrillingly controversial in the racy, sensationalist sexual behaviours it depicted. Both Blanche's promiscuity and Allan Grey's tortured homosexuality would have shocked the conservative audiences of mid-20th Century America, not to mention Stanley's appalling sexual violence. Additionally, there is also the frankness about discussing the nature of sexual desire in marriage itself. No wonder the critic C.W.E. Bigsby described it as 'the first American play in which sexuality was the core of the lives of all its principal characters.'[13]

The undoubted star of the original Broadway show was Marlon Brando, then an unknown 23-year-old actor, just starting out on his journey to becoming one of the most important actors of the 20th Century, an actor who 'gave us our freedom,' according to Jack Nicholson. Brando's naturalistic, and radically new, Method acting crashed up against the more classical acting style of British actress Jessica Tandy as Blanche, causing a type of performance conflict that fed beautifully into the play's central conflict. Brando was too young to match the Stanley of Williams' play but Williams himself thought that Brando brought something that redeemed Stanley a little: 'the brutality or callousness of youth.'[14] In other words, Stanley is so destructive because he's immature and hasn't learned to grow up yet. Maybe. Early audiences hoovered this up, laughing along with Stanley's comic barbs at Blanche and seemingly siding with the aggressor rather than the protagonist, much to Tandy's outrage. While Tandy received glowing reviews [Brooks Atkinson in *The New York Times*: 'it does seem almost incredible that she can convey it [her performance] with so many shades and impulses that are accurate, revealing and true'[15]], it was Brando's searing performances that audiences came for. Richard Watts Jr, in a *New York Post* review, praised Brando's

---

[13] C.W.E. Bigsby, *Modern American Drama 1945 to 1990.*

[14] Tennessee Williams, quoted in Claudia Roth Pierpont, *Method Man* in The New Yorker, October 2008.

[15] Brooks Atkinson, *The New York Times*, December 1947.

'portrayal of the heroine's sullen, violent nemesis as an excellent piece of work'.[16] Kirsten Shepherd-Barr argued that 'Brando made it Stanley's play, whereas [Williams' original playscript and] later productions emphasised Blanche'.[17] Of course, Brando's movie-star good looks certainly helped too, especially in the film version. All-in-all, Brando casts a shadow of deepest dark over every Stanley that followed, and will follow him, especially because his performance has been captured on film.

Kazan's 1947 production jettisoned the more Expressionistic flourishes of Williams' original stage directions, especially the lurid shadowy shapes that flame up the walls as Blanche mentally disintegrates. Wolcott Gibbs, in *The New Yorker*, described it as 'a fine and deeply disturbing play, almost faultless in the physical details of its production and the quality of its acting'. Gibbs also praised Joel Mielziner's highly effective stage set, which he described as a 'gruesome interior' characterised by 'decaying horror' through its 'sparse and dreadful' furnishings. Brooks Atkinson was more restrained but also complimented 'the shadowy environment' Mielziner created to house Williams' 'poignant and luminous story'.[18] Bess Rowen describes the set as creating a space that 'looked both grim and imposing and artificially contained, mirroring Blanche's feelings towards her setting'.[19]

However, it wasn't all gushing praise. Gibbs had reservations about the 'incredible" aspects of the plot, concerned that Blanche's fall from Belle Reve leisure lady to mentally unstable down-and-out was 'a good deal more picturesque than probable,' feeling that 'her degradation is much too rapid and complete.'[20] Whereas Susannah Clapp, in a 2014 *Guardian* review, called it 'one of the most glorious switchback plays ever written', most of the early criticism was aimed at the structure of the play. While some critics complained

[16] Richard Watts Jr., *The New York Post*, December 1947.

[17] Kirsten Stephen-Barr, *The Connell Guide*.

[18] Wolcott Gibbs, *The New Yorker*, December 1947.

[19] Bess Rowen, Introduction to *A Streetcar Named Desire*.

[20] Wolcott Gibbs, The New Yorker, December 1947.

about its episodic structure and refusal to stick to a tighter, more conventional form, the darkness of the content also provoked objections. The violence, the urban squalor, the sexual frankness and predatorial, coarse and boorish antagonist all contributed to an 'almost desperately morbid turn of mind', according to Richard Watts Jr.[21] J.C. Trewin went a lot further calling the play 'a squalid anecdote of a nymphomaniac's decay in a New Orleans slum'[22] - harsh! The pessimistic ending didn't help either: the protagonist is ravaged, sexually and mentally, and stumbles out of the play into oblivion; her sister commits her to an asylum, while deluding herself about her rapist husband; and finally, the sexual predator escapes punishment, being rewarded with a devoted wife and a new baby son.

A *Streetcar Named Moderate Desire*: The 1951 Film Version

The first thing that Warner Brothers had to tackle was that ending. Hollywood audiences were unused to the type of pitch-black ending found in the original play and to complicate things the film censorship board, known as the Breen office, had major issues with the murky morality of the play and its frank openness about sexual desire. More of which later. Warner Brothers took on the project, recruited Elia Kazan as director, reprising his theatrical role, and also employed Williams to write the screenplay, which is essentially the playscript pruned to feature film length. However, Warners had a problem. The Broadway actors were silver screen nobodies: they needed star power. Enter stage left, Vivien Leigh, Academy award winning actress and screen beauty. Aged 26, she had starred in the role of Scarlett O'Hara in 1939's *Gone with the Wind*. This role meant that in American popular culture Leigh came to be seen as *the* archetypal Southern Belle. Hence her screen performance as Blanche seemed to embody the seemingly inevitable decline and decay of the South itself.

At the time of filming *Streetcar...* she was 37, a perfect casting choice for the role of the fading belle. She had also played this part in Lawrence Olivier's

---

[21] Richard Watts Jr., *The New York Post*, December 1947.

[22] J.C. Trewin, *The illustrated London News*, 1949.

London production of the play in 1949. While most of the old crew were back, Leigh's inclusion meant the rejection of the original Broadway Blanche, Jessica Tandy, who was hurt by this development, especially after the very positive reviews of her performance. Marlon Brando had always thought Tandy miscast as Blanche, preferring Leigh's more openly sexual interpretation of the character. However, while this sexually focused performance ran closer to the play, it was problematic for the film.

The original screenplay created significant issues with the film censors, which necessitated a toning down of Blanche's nymphomania [the censor's expression], an obfuscation of Allan Grey's homosexuality and an artistic symbolising of Blanche's rape trauma. This refining of the playworld's manners is seen right away with an extremely polite, well-spoken sailor, who helpfully assists Blanche onto the streetcar named desire, rather than bawling at Eunice about the whereabouts of the nearest stripclub/brothel! The carnal desires of Stella, especially Kim Hunter's lust-filled facial expression when reconciling with Stanley after the poker game, and of Mitch are much reduced in temperature, either through editing of the original footage or at the screenwriting stage. Meanwhile, Allan Grey's suicide is the film is driven by Blanche's disgust at his 'weakness' for being a poet. So, the 'degenerate' Stella criticises in the original play disappears behind the film screenplay. However, despite the 4 minutes cut from the original version, the film version more than captures the maelstrom of sexual energies engulfing the characters.

In general, the film version captures the chaotic din of the French Quarter, the sultry heat and throbbing noise, the overcrowded pleasure-seeking focus of the place. In the film, Kazan could move outside of the claustrophobic confinement of the Kowalski apartment to reveal exterior shots of the train station, streets, and a lake, as well as going inside into bowling alleys and the production plant, where Mitch and Stanley work. Obviously, this eschewed the Expressionist visual elements of the play, but the realism of the set captured the cramped space of the apartment, filling it with small furniture and lots of props to emphasise the lack of privacy for all involved. The use of both diegetic and non-diegetic sound is brilliant, especially whenever Blanche is forced to revisit the Allan Grey tragedy. Stanley's simple enquiry about it when they first meet sounds far-away and echoing, suggesting her mental fragility. Her inability to deal with reality is also shown cleverly in the lighting of her reunion with Stella in the bowling alley. An overhead conditioning fan creates the visual effects of shadowy blades attacking her, in a way that makes her appear overwhelmed and vulnerable, feeding into the wider narrative strategy of light being a bad thing. See also the amplification of the passing locomotive, which is deafening in the film, when the two sisters are quarrelling about the loss of Belle Reve.

Kazan saw the film as an opportunity to rebalance the original Broadway production, which he thought became Stanley's play, rather than Blanche's. Whereas Brando dominated the play and relegated Tandy to a sort of major minor character, Kazan was able to use the camera to prise the audience's gaze away from Brando in a way the theatre audience simply couldn't, or wouldn't. The film restored the playscript's original vision by recentring Blanche and pushing Stanley more towards the margins.

Kazan uses film language very effectively to capture the central relationship of the two. What is most striking about the film is how Kazan captures Blanche's female gaze, Leigh's facial expression hungrily taking in Stanley's

muscular physique on several occasions, especially when Brando takes off his sweat-drenched T-shirt for the first time. In their first encounter, Brando is shown at a slightly lower angle and closer up than Leigh, who is filmed from a slightly higher angle and from further away. Stanley fills the screen and looks down on Blanche, whereas she appears more vulnerable in the glare of his masculine domination. There's also something more mesmerically modern about Stanley, with his shiny bomber jacket that relegates Blanche's floaty, prissy outfits to outdated obsolescence. He's sleek and future-facing; she appears backwards and out of touch. Despite this, Stanley's boorishness is undeniable, whether through his violent words and arguments, or whether through smaller actions like the fact he always seems to be eating with his gob stuffed full of food!

Whereas it was possible for theatre audiences to side with Stanley, the censors ensured that there was no such moral ambiguity in the film. Moral complexity was suffocated at the screenwriting stage so that it is blatantly clear that Stanley cannot be rewarded with a loving, subservient wife and newborn son. A rapist simply cannot be gifted a family, according to 1950s film law. Whereas the play ended with Stella choosing to disbelieve her sister's accusations of rape and succumbing to Stanley's sexual magnetism, in the film she emphatically rejects him. However, it is only with the painful, melodramatic handover of Blanche to the doctor that Stella finally sees her husband's cruelty for what it is: unadulterated sadism. Her 'Don't ever touch me again!' is such a huge denunciation of what's gone before, and is reinforced by her running upstairs to Eunice's apartment with her newborn son. In a clever echo of the earlier 'STELL-LAHHHHH!' scene, this time Stanley is left bellowing and bereft, rejected and judged, not only by his wife but his entire community. Notably Pablo and Steve stare at him accusingly and with disgust as Blanche is escorted off the premises, necessitating Stanley having to defend himself: 'I never touched her!' The film may end with his anguished roars, but the film audience leaves the cinema comforted by the knowledge that his calls will not be answered. He has been well and truly punished.

A Racecar Called Desire: BIPOC Productions

American productions with all-black casts have been staged frequently and from quite soon after the initial 1947 production. As early as 1953, all-black productions tackled the story, which necessitates subtle reformulations of the social dynamics of the play. How does an audience process the tale of an unstable white woman who hails from a plantation-owning dynasty played by a black actress? What does the director do with the play's emphasis on Stanley's 'Polack' status, a man descended from white immigrant heritage? The concept of colour-blind casting in drama productions is surely a positive development to create better opportunities for actors outside the narrow white mainstream, but regardless of how colour-blind a production might be, this doesn't necessarily create a colour-blind audience.

Williams' play may depict an 'easy intermingling of the races' but in reality, it is a white play with tokenistic gestures to multiracial diversity. Pablo is a bit-part poker player, the unnamed 'Negro Woman' who chats to Eunice is a friendly, if lascivious drunk, the 'Mexican Woman' selling flowers for the dead is a threatening presence to Blanche [particularly in the 1951 film, which shows her as a stalking, shadowy silhouette]. Race exists, but only on the margins of the play and also in fleeting, limited glimpses - only Pablo is given the complexity of a name!

Bess Rowen points out the dangers of handing Stanley to a black actor, where his antagonist role, brutish domination of others, domestic violence, casual cruelty and especially his dangerous sexual charge can perpetuate 'harmful stereotypes that were established during the time of slavery and were continued through racist forms of American theatre such as minstrelsy'.[23] Of the two male leads, only Mitch has a character than avoids perpetuating reductive racial stereotypes. Steve and Eunice could easily be played by BIPOC actors without any serious problems. The easiest solution regarding this racial complexity is to choose an all-BIPOC cast. In an American context, it would be interesting to consider the effect of casting certain roles for black actors and others for native American actors. For example, what impact would there be if casting a native American man as Stanley, or Blanche and Stella as Asian-Americans? Again, such alternative casting choices would require careful, nuanced consideration to enrich rather than aggravate American racial politics.

In 2018 the African American Shakespeare Company in San Francisco staged an all-black *Streetcar...* which saw Jemier Jenkins play Blanche and Khary Moye take on Stanley. Sophie Kim's review of the play in The Daily Californian pointed to a fresh recalibration of the comic potential of the play. Director L. Peter Callender's version was 'saturated in comedic devices'.[24] While clearly a strategy to update and realign the play for 21st Century audiences,

---

[23] Bess Rowen, Introduction to *A Streetcar Named Desire.*

Callender's production attempted to laugh the audience past some of the obvious contradictions of a white playwright's 1947 play pondering the crumbling American South through an all-black casting. Practically speaking, an all-black production needs to decouple the play from its original 1947 setting and embrace a fresher 21st Century setting, where the idea of two sisters from a wealthy black background losing a massive country mansion is more credible. Rowen also discusses an all-black Broadway production from 2012 that excised the racist 'Polack' term from the play, removing completely any considerations of racial politics from audience responses. No matter how they're done, BIPOC productions of the play, or productions that mix BIPOC actors with white actors, need to be highly sensitive to the optics of race, to avoid unhelpful distortions and distractions.

A Queercar Named Desire: The Belle Reprieve Production, 1991

Thomas P. Adler points out that the central relationship between Blanche and Stanley is not one of simplistic binaries, where Stanley is merely the Anti-Blanche and vice versa. He explains that rather than being mutually exclusive opposites, their personalities exhibit a fascinating Venn diagram of similarities. Adler claims that 'there is a Blanche side to Stanley'[25] and, conversely, a Stanley side to Blanche. Blanche is not only sexual prey but also a predator and similarly Stanley too is not just a brutish man but also a vulnerable, abandoned boy. Several critics have highlighted this unusual character androgyny and even Williams himself claimed that Blanche was a version of himself, as well as suggesting that he also possessed elements of Stanley. It is at the intersection of this complex and unusual character fluidity and the playwright's own personality that fuelled the wild imaginative reinterpretation of Streetcar... by Split Britches and Bloolips in 1991. This radical queer adaptation of the play saw the theatre companies build upon Carla McDonagh's ideas that both Blanche and Stanley are consummate actors, delivering exaggerated performances, or 'masquerades' of gender:

Stanley, the hypermasculine ape and Blanche, the chaste Southern belle.[26]

The *Belle Reprieve* production turns the play on its head to explore gay and lesbian sex in the 1940's. This celebration of queer desire saw Stanley become a butch lesbian; Stella became a femme lesbian or 'a woman disguised as a woman'; Blanche, appropriately, was transformed into a drag queen or 'a man in a dress', while Mitch was played as a 'fairy disguised as a man'. It presents an intoxicating array of alternative sexualities and gender roleplaying, highlighting the liberation of fluid sexual and gender identities, in contrast to the narrow confinement of heterosexual binary opposites. It also burrows into the idea of how a homosexual playwright's representations of heterosexual desire may distort those desires, refracting them through a highly unusual imaginative prism to create a type of unique crossdressing spectacle. While the production created much humour through the comic confusion of this new playworld and its knowing nods to the original play, Clara Abbott's analysis of *Belle Reprieve* suggests that Blanche in the original play is notably othered, or fundamentally and profoundly queer, in her inability to fit into the narrow patriarchal sexual values of mid-20th Century America. Her preference for magic over realism, her inability to separate past from present and certainly her inability to form a viable future in this world marginalises her in a way akin to alternative, queer identities in the same period. Abbot interprets the poignant musical solo sung by this new drag-Blanche as begging 'the audience to understand Blanche's relationship to the past as no longer ridiculous or over the top but rather deeply melancholic'.[27]

All Them Coloured Lights [and Rock 'n' Roll]: Benedict Andrews Production, 2014

Benedict Andrews' 2014 production for the National Theatre in London was hugely successful for several reasons, one of them being the star-draw of Gillian Anderson as Blanche and another being Andrews' vibrant and exciting

---

[26] Clara McDonagh, quoted by Philip C. Kohn, Williams: *A Streetcar Named Desire*.

[27] Clara Abbot, *Generations of Desire: Belle Reprieve and the 'Beautiful Dream' of Blanche Dubois*.

theatrical vision. A major innovation of the production was the use of a constantly revolving stage set within a theatre-in-the-round theatrical space. The apartment is a mere structural skeleton, allowing the audience to see into its every corner. Even the translucent curtain that divides the bathroom from the rest of the apartment reinforces the idea that privacy is impossible, an inconvenience that amplifies the tensions between the characters. It's an interesting stagecraft decision, in that it captures the complete lack of privacy that the characters must endure in the cramped space but also truth becomes a constantly shifting, almost customised, concept for each individual audience member. Obviously, this needs very careful choreography of the actors in their stage movements, but it also has the additional benefit of needing the audience to lean into the stage action, trying to gain the best view from their vantage point. Interestingly, the stage set only begins rotating after Blanche has her first sneaky drink of Stanley's liquor, subtly externalising the mental chaos of her mind.

Anderson's Blanche doesn't appear too moth-like in her sophisticated ivory dress suit, heels and large sunglasses but she plays her with a giddy energy that suggests nervousness or agitation. Immediately, it is clear that Blanche is an expert actor, who knows that the right performance for the right person means gaining advantage. Anderson plays this to the point of parody - an over-the-top accent, a long-drawn out drawl, exaggerated gestures and facial expressions - all maximise the play's comic potential. Visually the sisters are as different as can be: Blanche is blonde, Stella is brunette; Stella is tall and slender, Blanche much more petite. Costume is also cleverly used to differentiate between the sisters: Stella's much more casual yet striking yellow and blue attire shows how different they have become. This costume strategy is continued throughout the play. When the sisters prepare to go to Galatoire's, Stella's dress is notably shorter, more youthful, more French Quarter than Blanche's more respectable but more old-fashioned attire.

The opening of the production is enjoyable and full of humour; it is good at delivering the comedy in the playscript - Blanche's comment about Stella being 'as plump as a little partridge' is played for laughs, given Vanessa Kirby's slender, statuesque figure. Blanche is portrayed as an attention-seeking annoyance and, while comic, it comes close to turning the audience against her - we begin to endure her too and identify with Kirby's weary facial expressions.

Andrews uses the transitions between scenes to inject attention-grabbing dosages of lurid colour and loud rock music. It is exciting, disorientating and practical: while the audience is distracted by this sensory overload the actors get on with changing costumes or rearranging the set. The juxtaposition of the realistic stage action and the more Expressionist scene transitions is sudden and loud, a type of sensory violence that is reflected in the decision to explicitly stage the domestic violence of Scene 3. The assault on Stella is truly shocking. Whereas the 1951 film partially obscured the violence by using a carefully placed camera to show Stanley but not Stella and the original playscript hides it behind a wall, Andrews' production stages it in the kitchen and in plain sight. The explosion of chaotic movement, the bright lighting and Kirby's distressed movements, together with the blood streaming from her nose are provocative. The extremity of this violence is mirrored by the intensity of their reconciliation, and it makes for potent, heady drama. Andrews' production also takes more risks with clothing with both Kirby and Foster scantily clad in their underwear on stage at times. As opposed to the 1951 film, which skips forward to Kim Hunter glowing in post-coital bliss the morning after, Andrews boldly stages their reconciliation as a sexual battle for domination, all soundtracked by P.J. Harvey's abrasive 'To Bring You My Love'. The fact that the audience can see this highly sexual reunion and that Mitch and Blanche converse outside the door while it happens renders it both powerful and uncomfortably voyeuristic. Regardless, it certainly portrays to Blanche the powerful sexual chemistry between her sister and her husband.

The struggle between protagonist and antagonist runs along familiar lines, but there are some nuances. Blanche's tirade about Stanley being an ape in Scene 4 is notable for being played for laughs while still retaining its menace. Ben Foster's facial expression is one of genuine pain as he hears her stream of insults, but his menace is clear at the end of the scene; the scene seems to give him the motivation to pursue Blanche with such clear-headed cruelty later in the play. Michael Billington stated that 'there is something dangerous about this sweaty, tattooed, close-cropped Stanley who has recently been discharged from the military and who has not lost his combative instinct'[28] but, through his tone of voice, Foster still maintains an air of vulnerability, allowing an audience to understand his side of things. The halting way Foster delivers some of his lines also makes Stanley seem more unsure of himself, certainly much less cocksure than Brando in 1951, almost as if he knows he's being unreasonable but that he's being pushed to this by his provocative and wearying sister-in-law. When he talks to Stella about the way he's treated Blanche there's an undercurrent of appeal to his wife, imploring her to understand how he had no other choice.

Despite arguably allowing this audience empathy of Stanley's plight, Andrews ensures that Blanche's pathetic derangement in Scene 10 forbids any siding with Stanley. Blanche is a mess of lace and sequins and her ill-fitting ballroom dress, complete with smeared lipstick make her look truly unhinged. Anderson's jerky body movements and her frenzied gestures appear simultaneously like a spoilt little girl throwing a tantrum and an old woman stumbling in a storm. As in the 1951 film, the rape scene is an unnerving mix of the symbolic and the realistic. It carries overtones of exploitation, of an opportunist man taking advantage of a woman too drunk to defend herself. Foster's pulling up of Anderson's layers of underskirt netting is deeply disturbing, especially as he does this looking like an ape, visually delivering Blanche's prophecy of ending up with the apes. In the finale, Blanche's complete destruction is shown visually in her dishevelled appearance, all lank hair, no make-up and looking utterly exhausted. Additionally, Kirby's portrayal of Stella when Blanche is lead away to the asylum is one of pure anguish and unendurable pain; it is extremely affecting drama. All of which ensures that the tragedy of this silly, vain, soft woman runs like razor wire over the audience's skin.

---

[28] Michael Billington, *The Guardian*, July 2014.

Analysing an extract

If you're studying the play at GCSE level, it's likely that you'll be expected to analyse an extract in exam conditions. The question is likely to be along the lines of 'explore how Williams makes this extract dramatically compelling'. Our strong advice is not to work through the extract from start to end, however tempting that might be, because doing so will encourage you to summarise what happens rather than focusing, as the question requires, on Williams' dramatic technique. So, instead, choose three or four major aspects and write a paragraph on each of these.

Always keep in mind that when you are analysing any specific detail of the extract, such perhaps as a particular word or phrase used by a character, you need to explain how this is significant in terms of the play as a whole. You are not simply being asked to produce a linguistic task; through analysing the language you are required to demonstrate your knowledge and understanding of the whole text, including what happens in it and its thematic concerns – desire, illusion, loneliness and so forth. In the light of this, it is also important to make brief references to scenes, lines, moments in the rest of the play throughout your essay.

Extract from Scene 2

STANLEY: Where's the papers? In the trunk?
BLANCHE: Everything that I own is in that trunk.
[*Stanley crosses to the trunk, shoves it roughly open and begins to open compartments.*]
BLANCHE: What in the name of heaven are you thinking of! What's in the back of that little boy's mind of yours? That I am absconding with something, attempting some kind of treachery on my sister?-- Let me do that! It will be faster and simpler.... [*She crosses to the trunk and takes out a box*] I keep my papers mostly in this tin box. [*She opens it.*]
STANLEY: What's them underneath? [*He indicates another sheaf of papers.*]

BLANCHE: These are love-letters, yellowing with antiquity, all from one boy. [*He snatches them up. She speaks fiercely*] Give those back to me!

STANLEY: I'll have a look at them first!

BLANCHE: The touch of your hands insults them!

STANLEY: Don't pull that stuff! [*He rips off the ribbon and starts to examine them. Blanche snatches them from him, and they cascade to the floor.*]

BLANCHE: Now that you've touched them I'll burn them!

STANLEY [*staring, baffled*]: What in hell are they?

BLANCHE [*on the floor gathering them up*]: Poems a dead boy wrote. I hurt him the way that you would like to hurt me, but you can't! I'm not young and vulnerable anymore. But my young husband was and I--never mind about that! Just give them back to me!

STANLEY: What do you mean by saying you'll have to burn them?

BLANCHE: I'm sorry, I must have lost my head for a moment. Everyone has something he won't let others touch because of their--intimate nature.... [*She now seems faint with exhaustion and she sits down with the strong box and puts on a pair of glasses and goes methodically through a large stack of papers.*] Ambler & Ambler. Hmmmmm.... Crabtree.... More Ambler & Ambler.

STANLEY: What is Ambler & Ambler?

BLANCHE: A firm that made loans on the place.

STANLEY: Then it was lost on a mortgage?

BLANCHE [*touching her forehead*]: That must've been what happened.

STANLEY: I don't want no ifs, ands or buts! What's all the rest of them papers? [*She hands him the entire box. He carries it to the table and starts to examine the papers.*]

In any extract from the play, there will be interesting aspects of **characterisation**. In this extract from Scene 2, we learn more about Blanche's back story and there are hints about her tragic marriage and the continued hold this has over her imagination. We also learn more about Stanley. Quickly seeing through Blanche's façade, he doesn't trust what she says and insists on reading the documentary evidence for himself. He doesn't care whether this material is sensitive or personal, he just wants to make sure that Blanche is not ripping off Stella and, through her, him too.

The **language** Williams gives both Blanche and Stanley conveys their contrasting characters. Whereas Stanley speaks characteristically in simple, straightforward language, mostly composed of Anglo-Saxon derived monosyllables, Blanche's language is more complex and cultured, reflecting her upper-class upbringing, and her projection of a self-consciously refined sensibility. Stanley opening questions, for instance, are both short and curt, composed of just three words each. The language reveals his aggressive impatience. He doesn't bother with niceties or waste time with politeness. He doesn't beat around the bush. He is direct and blunt and demanding, almost harrying Blanche with his questions. Blanche's sentences are noticeably much longer, use fancier words and tend to be exclamatory. Complex words such as 'absconding', 'treachery' and 'iniquity' are a natural part of her more elevated vocabulary.

Discussion of Blanche and Stanley's speech patterns and what these reveal about their personalities encourages us to consider the characters in terms of their **relationship** with each other. Taken from Scene 2, this extract is only the second time we have seen Blanche and Stanley alone together within the uncomfortably confined space of the flat. Indeed, Blanche has manufactured this private scene by sending her sister on an errand to fetch her a drink. In next to no time, the atmosphere between the two has become heated and tense. Stanley fires off a barrage of terse and intrusive questions. On the back foot, Blanche tries her best to answer him and to ease the tension. When she does try to assert herself, raising her voice to speak 'fiercely' and command him to give her love letters back, he just ignores her, informing her matter-of-factly that he'll 'have a look at them first'. Clearly already this is a power play and Stanley seems to have the upper hand.

As elsewhere in the play, the **stage directions** are very important. These directions confirm the impressions the dialogue have made of both Stanley's character and his attitude to Blanche. As he does elsewhere in the play, Williams uses violent verbs to describe Stanley's actions. Not waiting for her permission, Stanley goes to Blanche's trunk and violently 'shoves it open'. Then he 'snatches' the letters and 'rips' the ribbon off. Stanley has no respect for Blanche's personal possessions or for her, and, moreover, he is showing her he has no respect. In contrast to Stanley's violent vigour, Blanche soon becomes 'faint with exhaustion' and appears to give in to his every demand. Handing Stanley the whole box of legal correspondence about Belle Reve, Blanche seems to be beyond caring, almost keen to divest herself of the burdens of the past.

Discourse analysis

Discourse analysis is a way of reading texts drawn from linguistics. It takes the features of real-world language use, or discourse, and applies them to literary texts. In particular, insights drawn from a branch of sociolinguistics called conversation analysis can illuminate new dimensions of scripted dialogue when applied to plays or film scripts. Although there are lots of useful ideas from sociolinguistics, we're going to confine ourselves to the following four key ones:

1. Grice's maxims
2. How power is encoded in conversational behaviour
3. Ideas about gender and conversational behaviour
4. Accommodation theory.

1.
Among the most useful ideas from sociolinguistics for the purpose of analysing dialogue in scripts are Grice's four maxims. Although we are not formally taught how to take part in a conversation, most of us pick up the unwritten rules and follow them, more or less, most of the time. Grice's four maxims make these implicit rules explicit: The maxim of quantity outlines how we tend to try to say as much as possible, but without talking for too long and without too much detail; the maxim of quality indicates how there is an unspoken assumption that we will tell the truth or not give false information, unsupported by evidence; the third maxim is one of relation and indicates how we try to make our contributions to a conversation relevant to the topic at hand; the final maxim is that of manner, which indicates how we try to be as clear as possible, avoiding unnecessary obscurity.

Even a cursory flick through the pages of the play reveals many examples of where various characters break several of the maxims. Blanche, unsurprisingly, is the prime unspoken rule breaker, particularly when she is in conversation with her sister. Frequently Blanche dominates these conversations, talks for far longer in her conversational turn than is expected, leaves little room for

Stella to make contributions and also, frequently lies, breaking the maxim of quality.

2.

A second useful set of ideas from conversation analysis concern how power is established and developed within dialogue. There are several aspects showing how power operates within conversations. Firstly, there is who gets to talk first and who sets the conversational topic. However, conversations tend to develop, so setting the initial topic isn't necessarily an indication of power if other interlocutors challenge and change the topic. Hence control of the topics as the conversation unfolds is a more reliable sign of power. Sometimes too, who gets to have the last word, the final say, is significant.

Similarly, speaking the most and, in fiction, having the most lines can indicate power, but depends on how the speech is received by the other interlocutors. Sometimes withholding participation and the use of silence can be indicators of resistance and demonstrate power.

Turn-taking is another important feature of conversations, with the management of turns often significant. The term 'adjacency pairs' refers to a pattern whereby the utterance of the first speaker sets up an expectation of the kind of response appropriate from a second speaker A cordial greeting, for instance, sets an expectation for a similar sentiment in response. Breaking adjacency pairs thus indicates a small power play. Similarly butting in, cutting off and interrupting another speaker, rather than waiting for one's turn, is another small seizure of power.

The types of speech people use also conveys power relationships. A sophisticated vocabulary can indicate power, but so too can blunt monosyllables. Use of polite terms, such as sir or madam, can also be revealing, as can the absence of such terms.

Power is also encoded by which participants in a conversation get to ask the questions and which ones are obliged to answer. If a character asks questions and another character does not answer them, like silence, this can also reveal which of the two really holds the upper hand.

Similarly, who is allowed to pass judgements and whether these judgements are accepted are other good indicators of power dynamics.

3.

Linguists have long argued that men and women follow different unspoken rules in conversation. According to some researchers, broadly speaking, women follow a co-operative principle in conversation, whereas men follow a competitive one. For example, whereas women are more likely to use 'back-channel support', i.e. encouraging and supportive comments that chip in while another person is speaking, men are more likely to interrupt each other to take control of the topic. In mixed conversations, so the theory goes, women are more likely to moderate their language behaviour and to exhibit 'weak' language features. These include lessening the conviction of a statement by adding 'hedges' and the use of what linguists call 'tag questions' at the end of an utterance. For instance, 'that's a really good idea, probably, I guess, don't you think so?'

However, recent research has suggested that these 'weak' features are more a symptom of power imbalances than of gender. Plenty of evidence indicates that when men are placed in a situation of inferiority, they tend to exhibit the same language features once deemed to be essentially female.

4.

Accommodation theory explains people's tendency to adjust their language behaviour to match their circumstances and, particularly, to the person or people with whom they are conversing. When, for example, we are talking to posh people, we might adjust our accent and vocabulary to sound more like them. Similarly, we might go the other way if we feel we feel we are sounding too posh with other interlocutors. But just as likely is that the reverse will happen. Refusing to attune our speech to an interlocutor is an act of resistance, a rejection of social pressures to conform, a refusal to be judged in this way. Sometimes non-accommodation can be deliberately provocative, such as when a teenager at a family gathering refuses to use Standard English, despite parental expectations that they should. Or when a singer from a punk band uses a swear word on prime-time television.

What might these sociolinguistic concepts add to our analysis? In terms of the extract from Scene 2 reproduced earlier. we do not know who opened this conversation. If we look it up, however, we will see that actually it is Blanche who speaks first and, initially, she also sets the rather meandering agenda of the conversation. But once Stanley orders her to 'cut the re-bop', a powerfully blunt imperative, he seizes topic control and focuses the conversation entirely on the papers and what has happened to Belle Reve. Similarly, it might appear, superficially, that Blanche is dominating the conversation as she speaks the most, until we realise her turns are almost always responses to something Stanley has said, signalling that he, in fact, is leading the conversation.

Shifts in power can be illustrated through changes in the use of questions and to the pattern of adjacency pairs. Near the start of the conversation, Blanche asks Stanley whether it is possible that she 'was once considered to be – attractive?' There is a clear expectation for how he is meant to respond and even though Stanley doesn't oblige with a compliment, he does reply: 'Your looks are okay'. Once he is in the box seat, Stanley is the one asking the questions and each time he fires one off, Blanche is obliged to respond in exactly way he wishes:

STANLEY: What is Ambler & Ambler?
BLANCHE: A firm that made loans on the place
STANLEY: Then it *was* lost on a mortgage?
BLANCHE: [*touching her forehead*]: That must've been what happened.

Asking questions can indicate control. Asking lots of questions in quick succession can also indicate control, like in an interrogation. In this short exchange, Stanley rattles off eight questions, with almost all of his utterances interrogative in nature. But asking questions can also signal uncertainty or weakness. When a character asks questions that are completely ignored by their interlocutor, for example, it is a clear sign of a power imbalance. In her second utterance, Blanche asks three questions in a row. The first is so weak and indirect as a question it ends up as an exclamation. The second is almost rhetorical, despite the provocatively patronising phrasing. The third, however, is more direct and accusatory: 'That I am absconding with something, attempting some kind of teaching on my sister?' The ellipsis that follows [the three full stops in a row] is significant because it indicates that this time Blanche pauses to give time for Stanley to answer. And, of course, he doesn't. Completely ignoring all three of Blanche's questions, he just presses on with his own agenda. A clear indication that he is in charge.

Although Stanley doesn't actually interrupt Blanche, his short injections of a question at the end of each of her longer utterances function like interruptions. It isn't obvious, for instance, that Blanche has finished her first turn when she says 'I keep my papers mostly in this tin box', but Stanley immediately cuts in with 'What's them underneath?'

Is Stanley's language masculine and Blanche's feminine? Possibly. Certainly, Stanley's language is direct, terse, to the purpose and what linguists call 'message-orientated'. This conversation for him is a vehicle for finding out information and to show who's the boss; he is not engaging in polite chit-chat or offering any emotional support. He doesn't bother with any politeness terms and his conversational behaviour is aggressively competitive; he likes to dominate.

Possibly Blanche's conversational behaviour expresses femininity. She is on the backfoot and in the subordinate position in this conversation. Moreover, she accepts this position and doesn't try to wrest control of the conversation back from Stanley. Rather than letting it go, she could, for example, have pressed him further on the nature of his suspicions about Belle Reve. She also uses a mild, genteel form of expletive – 'what in the name of heaven' – as well as a subtle hedge, saying 'that must've been what happened'. Sharp as a tack, Stanley picks this uncertainty up in his response, which is a declarative functioning as a command: 'I don't want no ifs, ands or buts'.

However, to come to reliable conclusions we'd need to draw on wider data, examining further examples of the ways in which Stanley and Blanche habitually communicate with other characters. The features we've identified above as possible examples of gendered conversational behaviour, could just as easily be attributed to class. Stanley uses language in this unadorned and functional way because he actively rejects the conversational niceties he associates with upper-class Southern snobs like Blanche. Not for him polite turn-taking, the use of terms of endearment or the avoidance of swearing or coarseness. He does not admire correct grammar or fine phrasing. He doesn't see these as markers of distinction. But he knows full well that other people do. Stanley's use of language is urban – it's dynamic, efficient, gets things done quickly, it cuts the bull. In contrast, Blanche's more leisurely, self-consciously decorative, often circumlocutory way of speaking, from his point of view, expresses a superiority complex and a decadent effeteness that is repellent.

As we've seen, Blanche and Stanley's conversational behaviour and their language does not accommodate to some sort of happy medium between them. Using terms from this aspect of sociolinguistics, Blanche does not 'downwardly converge' to sound more like Stanley and neither does he 'upwardly converge' either. In fact, they both refuse to make any accommodation at all. Not only do they not attune their language to each other in any way, their speech patterns actually become more distinctly different when they are together. Compare, for instance, Stanley's conversations with Stella. This is just another example of how Blanche and Stanley are presented as hostile opposites, constantly needling and provoking each other, refusing to accommodate each other's presence in any way in Stella's life.

Teaching & revision ideas

1. Before reading the play, watch the short film *The Departure*, by Gillian Anderson. Identify the story arc. What seems to be happening? Who are the people seen/heard in the film? Consider why the film has this title.

2. After reading the play, watch the film again. Try to match the events from the film with the revelations in the play about Blanche's life in Laurel.

3. The higher order skills of understanding and appreciation of a text need the solid base of textual knowledge, but the latter should not be mistaken for the former. There are plenty of different ways to help students consolidate their knowledge of *Streetcar*.... Here are a few suggestions:

    i.   Williams only gave one scene in the play a title. Individually pupils can devise their own titles for each scene and then, through comparison with those their peers have created, decide as a group on the best ones. Our titles can be found a little later in this guide.

    ii. Similarly, choosing one quotation as a title for each scene really focuses attention what is most significant and helps pupils to retain key quotations.

    iii. Writing one sentence summaries of each scene is helpful. Even more useful is to scramble up the order of these sentences and see how quickly pupils can arrange them in the right sequence.

4. Focusing on quotations is an incisive way to enhance textual knowledge, and at the same time develops appreciation of language and of characterisation.

    i.   Quotation quests turn learning quotations into a game and make excellent starters to lessons. Pick around 10 quotations. Read each one in turn. Pupils have to identify the speaker, the addressee or the character being spoken about, and the scene. 1 point for each. 5 points if they get all three. Here are a few to get you started:

- 'Don't play so dumb. You know what! – Where's the papers?'
- 'I am not a Polack. People from Poland are Poles, not Polacks.'
- 'I hadn't seen him again until last Christmas. I ran into him on Biscayne Boulevard. Then – just now – this wire – inviting me on a cruise of the Caribbean!'
- 'Those are inexpensive furs that Blanche has had a long time.'
- 'And diamonds! A crown for an empress!'
- 'A man with a heavy build has got to be careful of what he puts on him so he don't look too clumsy.'
- 'This game is seven-card stud.'
- 'I didn't know anything except I loved him unendurably but without being able to help him or help myself. Then I found out. In the worst of all possible ways.'
- 'Why, the Grim Reaper had put up his tent on our doorstep!'
- 'But there are things that happen between a man and a woman in the dark – that sort of make everything else seem – unimportant.'

ii.   Now pupils can focus on each quotation and explain in as much detail as possible what the language reveals about each speaker.

iii.   Variations of quotation quest include asking the pupils to pick the quotations themselves and one in which the teacher mixes genuine quotations from the play with fake ones. The game is the same as above, but with the added element of trying to spot the fakes. A final fun iteration is to ask the pupils to make up their own quotes imitating the speech patterns of the characters.

- 'I'm looking for my sister, Stella Dubois. I mean – Mrs Stanley Kowalski.'
- 'It was because – on the dance-floor – unable to stop myself – I'd suddenly said – 'I know! I know! You disgust me….''

- 'Well, this somebody named Shaw is under the impression he met you in Laurel.'
- 'You're both mistaken. It's Della Robbia blue. The blue of the robe in the old Madonna pictures.'
- 'But when she was young, very young, she had an experience that – killed her illusions!'
- 'Come on Blanche – for Christ's sakes – when ya gonna get out that damn bathroom?'
- 'Are you boxed out of your mind?'
- 'Flamingo? No! Tarantula was the name of it! I stayed at a hotel called The Tarantula Arms.'
- 'Thousands and thousands of years have passed him right by, and there he is – Stanley Kowalski – survivor of the Stone Age!'
- 'Oh, I don't like to get so close to a bright light - it's just, so exposing - why, it makes me feel like I've got no clothes on at all.'

5. Opinion spectrum - the teacher gives the class a controversial statement about a character or theme and pupils have to place themselves at one end or the other from strongly agree to strongly disagree. Each pupil then defends his/her position and pupils can, if they wish, move up or down the line.

6. Stage directions - focus on Williams' detailed visual descriptions of setting, costume, lighting etc. and ask pupils to sketch/find pictures of these and create a 'mood board' reflecting a particular scene or the whole play.

7. Analyse an extract, for example one of Blanche and Stanley's first exchanges, and identify the techniques Williams uses to show the changing balance of power, e.g. looking for distribution of dialogue, interruptions, types of sentences etc. and how they affect audience perception.

8. Allocate two pupils per part. Perform a scene with one actor reading the script and the other one saying what they might really mean.

9. Thought-tracking: Take any section of the dialogue and pick three moments to freeze the action. For each of these moments write what you imagine each character is really thinking.

10. Opposites attract! Write defence statements which run counter to the standard views of the main characters. For example, 'Stanley is victimised and belittled by the DuBois sisters and deserves our sympathy.' Or 'Stella is a doormat who should show some backbone'. Or 'Blanche is an immoral fantasist who gets what she deserves'. Now turn the statements into as many paragraphs as you can manage.

11. Reputedly, Williams loathed Margaret Mitchell's epic novel Gone with the Wind. Watch the trailer for the film and compare the depiction of the South in the film and the play. Also worth comparing are the characters of Scarlett O'Hara [red and feisty] with the ethereal Blanche.

12. All plays have 'shadowplays', the scenes the playwright chose not to dramatise, but are implied. For example, the scene where Blanche is reprimanded by the school inspectors once her relationship with the boy is discovered. Others include: Mitch and Blanche's date at the funfair; Stanley and his friends at the bowling alley; Blanche's first night at the asylum.

i. Identify as many of these scenes as you can in ten minutes.
ii. Consider why Williams didn't dramatise this scene.
iii. Choose one and write the playscript for it.

Possible scene titles

1. Arriving in Elysian Fields
2. The Napoleonic Code
3. The Poker Night
4. Darling Shep vs. Brutish Stanley
5. The Paper Lantern
6. Could it be – you and me Blanche?
7. The Flamengo Hotel
8. The Birthday Ticket
9. A Good, Plain Look
10. A Date from the Beginning
11. The Kindness of Strangers.

GLOSSARY

ALIENATION EFFECT – coined by German playwright, Berthold Brecht, it reverses the conventional idea that audiences suspend their disbelief when watching a play

ANTITHESIS – the use of balanced opposites, at sentence or text level

APOSTROPHE – a figure of speech addressing a person, object or idea

ASIDE – words spoken for only the audience to hear

CADENCE – the rise and fall of sounds in a line

CATHARSIS – a feeling of release an audience supposedly feels at the end of a tragedy

CONCEIT – an extended metaphor

DRAMATIC IRONY – when the audience knows things the on-stage characters do not

FIGURATIVE LANGUAGE – language that is not literal, but employs figures of speech, such as metaphor, simile and personification

FOURTH WALL – the term for the invisible wall separating the audience and the actors on the stage

GOTHIC – a style of literature characterised by psychological horror, dark deeds and uncanny events

HAMARTIA – a tragic or fatal flaw in the protagonist of a tragedy that contributes significantly to their downfall

HEROIC COUPLETS – pairs of rhymed lines in iambic pentameter

HYPERBOLE – extreme exaggeration

IAMBIC – a metrical pattern of a weak followed by a strong stress, ti-TUM, like a heart beat

IMAGERY – the umbrella term for description in poetry. Sensory imagery refers to descriptions that appeal to sight, sound and so forth; figurative imagery refers to the use of devices such as metaphor, simile and personification

JUXTAPOSITION – two things placed together to create a strong contrast

METAPHOR – an implicit comparison in which one thing is said to be another

METONYM – when something closely associated with a thing stands in for that thing, such as a book representing education

METRE – the regular pattern organising sound and rhythm in a poem

MONOLOGUE – extended speech by a single character

MOTIF – a repeated image or pattern of language, often carrying thematic significance

ONOMATOPOEIA – bang, crash, wallop

PENTAMETER – a poetic line consisting of fives stressed beats

PERSONIFICATION – giving human characteristics to inanimate things

PLOSIVE – a type of alliteration using 'p' and 'b' sounds

ROMANTIC – a type of poetry characterised by a love of nature, by strong emotion and heightened tone

SIMILE – an explicit comparison of two different things

SOLILOQUY – a speech by a single character alone on stage revealing their innermost thoughts

STAGECRAFT – a term for all the stage devices used by a playwright, encompassing lighting, costume, music, directions and so forth

STICHOMYTHIA – quick, choppy exchanges of dialogue between characters

SUSPENSION OF DISBELIEF – the idea that the audience willingly treats the events on stage as if they were real

SYMBOL – something that stands in for something else. Often a concrete representation of an idea.

SYNECDOCHE – when the part of something represents the whole, such as the crown for the British monarchy.

SYNTAX – the word order in a sentence. Syntax is crucial to sense: For example, though it uses all the same words, 'the man eats the fish' is not the same as 'the fish eats the man'

TRAGEDY – a play that ends with the deaths of the main characters

UNITIES – A description of a play's tragic structure by Aristotle that relates to three elements of time, place and action

WELL-MADE PLAY – a type of play that follows specific conventions so that its action looks and feels realistic.

About the authors

Head of English and writer, Neil Bowen has a Master's Degree in Literature & Education from the University of Cambridge and is a member of Ofqual's experts panel for English. He is the author of *The Art of Writing English Essays for GCSE*, co-author and editor of *The Art of Writing English Essays for A-level*, *The Art of Poetry*, *The Art of Literature* and *The Art of Drama* series. The ex-lead singer of a spectacularly unsuccessful Goth/punk/metal band, Neil regularly delivers talks at GCSE & A-level student conferences and occasionally CPD sessions for fellow teachers.

An Irish English teacher, Michael Meally holds an MA in American Literature as well as first class degrees in English Literature and Engineering. A champion crochetier, Michael is the co-author of *The Art of Writing English Literature Essays* and has contributed to many of the *Art of Poetry* and *Art of Drama* books.

Keen amateur bassoonist and dedicated campanologist, Sally Rowley is an experienced English teacher and Head of Sixth Form. Sally's particular interests include Chaucer, Jacobean and twentieth century drama, the musical legacy of Napalm Death and the history of root vegetables in England and Wales.

Lara Williams is an English teacher and former professional wrestler. Lara holds a degree in English Literature from Oxford University as well as a Guinness record for executing the most 'cobra clutch bulldogs' in a single bout of wrestling. When not reading a good book, Lara likes nothing better than tending her small flock or racing pigeons.

Printed in Great Britain
by Amazon

41506219R00108